Best
PUB WALKS
in and around
LEEDS

Colin Speakman

Published by Sigma Leisure – an imprint of
Sigma Press, 1 South Oak Lane, Wilmslow, Cheshire SK9 6AR, England.

British Library Cataloguing in Publication Data
A CIP record for this book is available from the British Library.

ISBN: 1-85058-451-6

Typesetting and Design by: Sigma Press, Wilmslow, Cheshire.

Cover photograph: The Garden Gate (by kind permission of Joshua Tetley & Son)

Maps: Neil Coates

Photography: Colin Speakman

Printed by: MFP Design and Print

was demolished when the railway was built across Leeds city centre in the 1860s. Only a section of facade remains (Walk 1), and the name White Hall Road, but nothing remains of the Coloured Cloth Hall which stood on the site now occupied by the Post Office in City Square.

Transport was a key to growth of both the textile and other trades, and a crucial development was transforming the River Aire into a waterway which could carry large enough vessels to transport bulk loads to the Humber ports and perhaps even across the North Sea. There were problems is using the river in terms not only of stretches of shallow water and rapids but places such as at Thwaite Mills and Leeds Dam where a weir was used to build up a head of water to drive a mill-wheel, but which also blocked the river to shipping. The answer was to create a "Navigation".

A Navigation is in effect a river which has been transformed by a series of improvements – deepening, straightening and new sections of "cut" to avoid such obstacles such as the many weirs which provided water power to drive the early mills. The Aire and Calder Navigation was sanctioned by Act of Parliament in 1699 and within a year the river was opened to commercial craft as far as Leeds Bridge, establishing Leeds as an inland port and trading centre and leading to its rapid industrial expansion as bulk supplies of raw material could be imported and goods exported. Constant improvements during the subsequent centuries – including work by the great engineer John Rennie – has kept the Navigation as a significant commercial waterway which continues to carry heavy cargoes – oil, coal, chemicals between Hull, Goole and the Humber ports, Wakefield, Leeds and Castleford with, since the 1960s, loads of up to 500 tons able to reach Leeds.

By the 1770s Leeds and Bradford merchants also recognised the need to have outlets to the Lancashire coast for the growing export trade via Liverpool to the New World, and work began on an ambitious project, the Leeds-Liverpool Canal which was to travel 127 miles across the Pennines, utilising the Aire Gaps and following the natural contours of the land to minimise the requirements for locks. Surveyed by John Longbotom of Halifax and built by teams of "navigators" or navvies from all over Britain and Ireland. It took a full 46 years to complete the route, owing to the financial crises of the Napoleonic Wars, but it was open as far as Skipton and Gargrave as early as 1771, linking Leeds with its wool-rich Dales hinterland, and providing supplies of limestone so essential to the iron and building industries. A superb engineering feat, it still required 844 feet ascending and descending through locks, fed by eight aqueducts and a mile and quarter of tunnels (Walks 7, 8, 9).

The opening of the canal system into Leeds was like lighting the blue touchpaper of the city's industrial expansion. By enabling large quantities of bulk supplies – coal, iron, limestone, chemicals to reach the centre of the city, it opened opportunity for the rapid growth of engineering and textile industries. In the 1790s a young mechanic arrived in Leeds to beg a night's lodging. Known as Matthew Murray, he was a gifted and highly innovative engineer. Within a few years he had developed new machinery for John Marshall's flax mill in Holbeck, invented machine tools, steam engines and in 1812 built two locomotives for John Blenkinsop's pioneering rack railway which ran from Middleton Colliery in Middleton Woods to wharfs near the Aire-Calder Navigation (Walk 2). Murray with his partners Fenton and Woods established the Round Foundry in Water Lane in 1797 and laid the foundation for Leeds, over the next two centuries, becoming a centre of excellence for engineering, including the building of traction engines and railway locomotives, which were exported throughout the world; an industry which has only ceased, through Central Government myopia, with the closure of Hunslet Locomotive works for manufacturing in 1995.

The rapid growth of heavy industry south of the river Leeds created a division of the city which still continues, as mill and colliery owners moved to the hillier country north of the city to escape the smoke, noise and blight of their activities south of the Aire. Fine Georgian and Victorian houses are still to be seen north of the city centre, many around elegant, leafy town squares. In Armley, Headingley, Farnley, Roundhay, large, once rural estates owned by great barons of industry such as the Gotts, Armitages or

Kitsons, or bankers such as the Nicholsons or Ingrams, now form some of the delightful public parks which are such a feature of Leeds and of several of the walks in this book.

Impressive public buildings such as the Town Hall, the Corn Exchange, Mechanics Institute, Public Library, Grand Theatre, and Market Hall reflect our forefathers' pride and confidence in the prosperous new city. Although a great deal of Georgian Leeds was destroyed in waves of later 19th century development, Leeds remains in form and scale an essentially Victorian city, developed to the scale of the pedestrian and not the car. A charming Victorian and Edwardian aspect which modern planners have correctly preserved and enhanced, is the system of arcades which was developed as a way of making better use of the narrow medieval courtyards off Briggate. What was done in effect was to roof over the alleyway with glass – a good way of keeping Yorkshire weather at bay – and developing sometimes twin storeys of shops in otherwise confined space. Excellent examples include Queens and Thornton Arcades, the County Arcade and the Grand Arcade. The new Victorian Quarter is a late 20th century attempt to emulate that Victorian town planning success.

The economic success of Leeds in the 19th century led to a rapid expansion of housing, sweeping away the old insanitary slums and expanding outwards into areas such as Harehills, Chapeltown and Kirkstall, developing a style of housing for which Leeds was at one time notorious, "back to back" terraces, ironically a style now much preferred to the modern sixties-style tower blocks. Improved urban transport played an important role in the process, at first suburban steam commuter railways to Bradford, York, Skipton, Otley, Ilkley, Wakefield, Dewsbury, Wetherby, and later along the streets, with horse buses and horse trams. By the end of the 19th century an extensive electric tramway network linked the city centre with such outlying suburbs as Headingley, Chapeltown and Stanningley. Trams, supplemented by trolley buses and motor buses in outlying areas, were cheap, efficient people movers. Between the Wars a whole new suburb of the city, out at Middleton and Belle Isle, was developed around the tramway system, with the Middleton Light

Railway (tramway) linking overspill sites by high quality public transport. Foolishly, the tramway system was, largely for ideological reasons, abandoned and demolished in the late 1950s, while most European cities were upgrading theirs. But in the closing years of this century, it is set to return with the coming of the Leeds Supertram a high quality, separate light rapid transit system, the first line, ironically, fairly close to where the excellent Bell Isle Trams used to run.

Ribbon development continued along the arterial roads and tramway routes, reaching out and absorbing many formerly independent townships such as Horsforth, Headingley, Whitkirk, Armley, Chapel Allerton, Rodley and Bramley districts that nonetheless still keep something of their independent character. The process has continued in the late 20th century with the extension of the Leeds City boundaries northwards into rural Wharfedale, taking in such towns as Otley, Wetherby, Guiseley, Aberford, Harewood and Bramham, and with them some magnificent Lower Dales countryside which form some of the most enjoyable parts of this book. This includes some of the great country house estates, such as Lotherton Hall (Walk 16), Bramham Park (Walk 18), Ledsham Park (Walk 19) in the curious but beautiful magnesium limestone countryside which cuts across Lower Wharfedale and Airedale, and gives the eastern fringes of the city distinctive, gentle rolling, richly wooded, deeply fertile countryside, more like southern England, landscapes that contrast sharply with gritstone valleys, mills and moorland fringed horizons of the west.

But topography has had another advantage. The steep-sided Pennine valleys, including Airedale itself and its tributary valleys, which characterise much of West and North Leeds, have, owing to their steepness, been difficult to develop for either housing or industry, and have remained in many cases extended strips of semi-natural countryside, oak and birch woods, green fingers into the heart of the city, usually with excellent footpaths along them. This is a very special aspect of Leeds and why so many of the walks in this book are, quite deliberately, linear rather than circular in format. Walks 4, 5, 6, 8, 12 especially explore such features.

Though buses replaced trams in the 1950s, the city has kept a good network of public transport, in recent years supplemented by improved and in some cases electrified local rail services. This again is invaluable for ramblers.

The biggest difference of the post war years is of course the growth of what the politicians used to call the "car owning democracy" – the rapid increase in the ownership and use of private cars, which by the 1960s were congesting the city centre. This has lead on the one hand to a vast proliferation of urban motorways and express-ways around the city, with huge areas being used for surface and multi-storey car parks. The dominance of private cars has been highly destructive of the environment in terms of loss of landspace, dislocation of communities. air pollution, noise, physical danger and visual damage – all aspects which, inevitably intrude on some otherwise fine walks in this book. On the other hand, Leeds has been a pioneer in city centre pedestrianisation, leading the way in the campaign to get cars out of the city centre streets and using new surfaces and street furniture to create a much better urban environment. Unlike the destructive 1960s, old buildings are being kept whenever possible to provide that essential continuity and new buildings such as the West Yorkshire Playhouse are designed in styles which are more sympathetic to the old fabric of the city.

Most remarkable of all perhaps, has been the transformation of the Leeds waterfront, the area around the river and canal basin where much of Leeds prosperity began, from a hidden area of neglect and despoilation, to one of private and public amenity. Through the joint efforts of Leeds Development Corporation and the City Council, the waterfront been opened up in a remarkable way, with decaying warehouses and factories transformed into modern office waterside accommodation and apartments, and new buildings erected in "post modernist" styles, generally using more sympathetic and traditional materials such as warm red brick and stone, to avoid the brutality of concrete oblongs of the 1960s and 70s – though enough of these remain to spoil the Leeds skyline.

So where is Leeds going in the next Millenium? The first point to make is that Leeds is now an Environment City, one of a handful of cities in Europe which is committed to new policies of sustainability and environmental improvement in terms of air and water quality, and better and safer environment, with a new stress on walking, cycling and public transport, with priority given to such "green" measures as improving air quality, recycling, housing improvement and the landscaping and renaturing of derelict areas to improve the quality of life of all its citizens. Traffic calming rather than traffic generating new roads is now on the agenda, though highway engineers inevitably claim that a few more roads and Inner-Loops need to be built to keep the traffic away from the centre. The city has a strong and dedicated Countryside Service which is doing a great deal of good work not only to keep rights of way open (and any problems on footpaths or trails in this book should be reported to the Footpaths Department 0113 232 6444) but to improve the quality of the Leeds countryside. The Parks in Leeds – several of which are utilised in the book – are exceptionally well cared for, and are features of which the city can justly be proud, giving green lungs to the city and opportunity which is available for everyone to enjoy. Parks such as Middleton Woods (Walk 2), Meanwood Park and The Hollies (Walk 5) Roundhay (Walk 6), Chevin Forest Park (Walk 14) and Lotherton Park (Walk 17) are exceptionally beautiful and all are celebrated in this book. Temple Newsam and Golden Acre richly deserved inclusion, but there wasn't the right pub in the right place for them to be included in a Good Pub Walks book.

Anyone interested in learning a little more about Leeds' development as a city, could do worse than look out Patrick Nutgens' *Leeds – the Back to Front, Inside out Upside Down City* (Stile 1979), or Peter Brears' excellent *Leeds Waterfront Heritage Trail* (Leeds City Museums 1993). Peter, former Director of Leeds City Museums and a remarkable historian of the city (he was the creator of the Museum of Leeds Trail), has also produced the outstanding *Images of Leeds 1850-1960* (Breedon Books 1992) which uses period photographs to explore many aspects of the city's growth and development.

The best available guide to the footpath network through Leeds' countryside is Douglas Cossar's excellent and very comprehensive *Ramblers' Leeds*, (Ramblers' Association, West Riding area, 1995), which has no less than 38 mainly circular walks and is packed with useful information.

Beer, Breweries and Pubs in Leeds

Like most parts of Britain, Leeds has benefited from the real ale revolution, that is the production of high quality, hand-pumped,cask beers. Not only has this meant that several small traditional brewers have survived, but one or two other small breweries have appeared if not in Leeds itself, at least in Yorkshire. CAMRA – the Campaign for Real Ale – locally and nationally, have kept a watchful eye on traditional beers in our region, and while generally the situation is good, they remain concerned about the many financial and other threats to traditional pubs and small breweries; most notably the amount of booze being imported from cross-Channel ports to evade British duty, and the determination of the big breweries to market pressurised, pasteurised keg beers, most notably the so-called "smooth" nitrokegs.

At the time of writing, real ale survives and even flourishes within West Yorkshire, and in Leeds in particular.

In fact, there are only two breweries currently functioning within the boundaries of Leeds – Tetley's, a massive international brewing combine, on Hunslet Lane, and the Fox and Newt – a tiny brew-house pub just off Burley Road, whose rather unusual brews are sampled in Walk 1.

Yet in practice, the real ale drinker and rambler has a surprisingly good choice of pubs. Inevitably, Tetley's dominates, and several, of the pubs in this book are Tetley's tied houses. Tetley's was established in Leeds by Joshua Tetley, a maltster from Armley who in 1822 took over William Sykes' brewery in Salem Place, Hunslet Lane. The company thrived and eventually acquired the larger site on Hunslet Lane close by that it still occupies. By 1864 Tetley's had developed capacity to brew up to 160,000 barrels a year. The celebrated Tetley Huntsman logo, with his monocle, still survives, though there are not many huntsmen or foxes in urban Hunslet where Tetley's is brewed. Over the years Tetley has acquired several other breweries, including its main Leeds rival Melbourne's, in 1962.

It now forms part of the Carlsberg-Tetley groups, and has a Warrington-based partner group, Tetley Walker. The distinctive dry, hoppy Tetley bitter, fruity Tetley Mild – at its best one of the great Milds of Britain – and slightly stronger and richer Imperial (a recent revival of a popular Victorian recipe) are classic Leeds beers, and generally warmly appreciated by Leeds Loiners – that is people Leeds born and bred – as a familiar part of the Leeds landscape. Generally Tetley's is an extremely good pint, not to be confused with the Warrington version found west of the Pennines which most Leeds drinkers don't rate very highly. The company have tried to keep many of their pubs in as close to the original state as possible, sometimes going to great trouble to keep the decor as it presumably was in the closing years of last cen-

Tetley head brewer Graham Simpson (left) and licensee Ronnie Stokes outside The Whip, Leeds. (Joshua Tetley & Son)

tury, and designating them as "Heritage" pubs. Inevitably, this is a book with a strong Tetley flavour!

Recognising that people like to look around breweries, Tetley's have gone a stage further with their Brewery Wharf Visitor Centre, along the riverside close to Leeds Bridge (Walk 1) which tells the story of brewing and beer from the Middle Ages to the present day, with a variety of exhibitions, and displays with the famous Tetley horses and drays, and presentations.

However, other brewers do get a share of the action in Leeds. To the east of Leeds, at Tadcaster on the River Wharfe, is the oldest brewery in Yorkshire, Samuel Smiths, still family-owned and brewing beer from local well water without any additives, (one of the few British beers to meet the exacting standards of the German Reinheitsgebot) fermenting the beer in Yorkshire stone square vats and keeping it in traditional oak casks. Sam Smith's Old Brewery Beer with its distinctive, slightly nutty flavour is a favourite for many people, and will appear along several of the walks in this book. Sadly, the slightly stronger and richer Museum Ale has now been discontinued by the company – at least in its cask form.

John Smith's, their rivals from Tadcaster, are owned by Courage and form part of the Courage national chain, but in recent years hand-pulled John's Smiths Bitter and Magnet Ale have improved immeasurably and are generally regarded as very acceptable by most people.

There are not many outlets in Leeds for that other favourite West Yorkshire independant brewery, Timothy Taylor's of Keighley, but the city does support one much-appreciated Timothy Taylor House, the Eagle Tavern on North Street, which offers Taylor's Bitter, Golden Best, Dark Mild and Ram Tam, and Landlord, (Walk 4), though Taylor's Landlord usually appears as a Guest Beer in the Duck and Drake and Cock o' the North (Walk 1).

Two other small independents with a strong regional allegiance and an excellent reputation are the Black Sheep Brewery, run by Paul Theakston of Masham, North Yorkshire where beer is brewed in the old Wellgarth Maltings in traditional Yorkshire slate square vats, and Old Mill Brewery from Snaith, Humberside. Several Leeds pubs now have Black Sheep Bitter or Special as a "permanent" guest ale, including the Town Hall (Walk 1) and Prince of Wales (Walk 7), while you'll usually find Old Mill Bitter in the Cock o' the North or Duck and Drake (Walk 1).

Whitbreads have a stronghold in Leeds having taken over Dutton's, brewers of OBJ and owners of the magnificent Kirkstall Brewery, (Walk 7) which was finally closed in 1983, but Whitbreads kept many of the former Dutton outlets. Whitbread pubs usually offer one or more of the nationally distributed but generally acceptable beers such Castle Eden and Boddingtons.

Scottish & Newcastle – generally trading as Youngers, own Theakston's, most of which is now brewed at Newcastle not at Masham. However, where Younger's and Theakston's are well-kept, for example at Whitelocks, central Leeds (Walk 1) or The Chequers Inn, Ledsham (Walk 19), it can be extremely good. Marston's Pedigree and Burton Bitter are regularly on tap as guest beers in the Leeds area and they are generally very acceptable to most beer drinkers.

It is of course, more than just good beer that makes a good pub, and there are many often quite subtle qualities that matter – friendliness of both staff and locals, including being welcoming to walkers who may arrive hot and sweaty out of the pouring rain, (though it's only good manners to take off very muddy boots if you're heading for a carpeted lounge), a pleasant atmosphere, cleanliness, reasonably priced food (including coffee or soft drinks for those not wanting alcohol), decor which may be a little scruffy or even ordinary but doesn't pretend to be what it isn't, without too much jukebox or fruit machine interference to a conversation (and preferably none) and, an important point for this book, some interesting countryside and footpaths on the doorstep.

Of course really what makes a good pub is a personal choice, one person's piece of paradise can be another person's nightmare. In any case, things can change, perhaps quickly, as landlords and pub managers and even breweries come and go with surprising speed. All this author can say is that when the research was done, in the Spring, Summer and early Autumn of 1995, that's how it was.

A point about opening times. These can vary, and while some indication is given about times, including reference to The Chequers at Ledsham which has a six-day licence, you might need to check, especially if wanting food. Though most pubs do provide food at lunchtime, there's nothing worse than arriving on a cold winter's day expecting hot food than to find that's the cook's day off – so a quick phone call (numbers indicated in the text) may save disappointment – and hunger.

Transport Matters

Every walk in this book is easily accessible by public transport.

There are three good reasons for this. At least 40% of us don't have access to a car, and this is book is for everyone. Cars cause additional congestion, pollution, noise, danger and visual impact in the countryside – and are at risk parked in lonely places – so the less they are used, the better. Thirdly, this is a book which encourages people to drink beer, and beer drinking and driving don't, and shouldn't mix. If you are driving, then ensure you stay well under the limit – or keep off the booze altogether, which is a pity because this is about beer and walking, and even if you have a non-drinking companion or driver in the party, that's a little unfair.

Moreover, a majority of the walks exploit the opportunity offered by public transport to undertake linear walks, easily the most satisfying kind of walk rather than having to return to the spot from where you began. This also reflects, as suggested earlier, the special qualities of Leeds' countryside.

Leeds has an excellent, inexpensive public transport network – supported by Metro, West Yorkshire Transport Authority, which covers the entire Metropolitan Borough. All the walks either start from railway stations where there is a frequent MetroTrain service, or from bus stops where there is at least a half hour bus service – sometimes more frequent than that, though Sundays can be less frequent and times should be checked.

Train times are available in the free MetroTrain leaflets or Metro-Train booklet, available from Leeds City station or the new Gateway

Yorkshire Information Centre at Leeds City Station. Bus times are available from the Metro office at Leeds Bus Station or you can phone the **Metro hotline** on 0113 245 7676 – leaflets for individual services will usually be sent by request. Most bus stops in the city and at outlying points have up-to-date timetable cases with information in simplified departure board format.

The excellent value Day Rover ticket in most cases is the ideal way of getting to and from every one of these walks. Valid on just about every bus and train in West Yorkshire, all day at weekends and Bank holidays, and after 0930 on weekdays, and valid as often as you like on as many different buses an trains as you choose, at time of writing it costs just £2.30 per adult, £1.15 per child and senior citizen, and £4 for a Family Card can be used for two adults travelling together and up to three children (or one adult and up to four children) – who don't have to be related. It's cheaper than petrol, but you must buy it in advance, from Leeds City or other staffed stations, Metro offices, Information Centres, local post offices and other outlets, and you must scratch off the day and month you are using it – like a Lottery card.

However, depending on how far you are travelling, it may be cheaper for a short single journey just to get an ordinary off-peak bus or Cheap Day Return rail ticket, costing as little as 60p. These are available after 0930 and before 1500 and after 1800 on weekdays, and all day at weekends and bank holidays.

Walk 1: A City Centre Amble

A stroll around the centre of Leeds to enjoy just a little of its rich architectural inheritance and history. No less than ten pubs well worth visiting are passed on the walkabout, but we strongly urge that you investigate them over several visits !

Distance: 3km (2 mls)

Maps: Pathfinder 683, and Leeds and Bradford A-Z Street Atlas.

Public Toilets: Public Utilities, Safeways, Bond Street; Corn Exchange, (basement).

Start & Finish: Leeds Town Hall

The Walk and The Pubs

Start at Leeds Town Hall, that magnificent mixture of classical colonnade and baroque designed by a hitherto unknown public competition-winning architect Cuthbert Brodrick from Hull and opened by Queen Victoria in 1858. Probably Britain's most famous town hall, used on television screens to symbolise local Government throughout Britain, this richly decorated architectural masterpiece with its attendant lions overlooking Victoria Square isn't in fact the seat of local Government, but is a civic space used for ceremony, public events and musical performances – including many a memorable oratorio. The real seat of power – Leeds City Council – is the Civic Hall, passed later on the walk.

Cross The Headrow at the traffic lights and turn right, soon reaching the **Town Hall** pub, a rather plain 1930s brick and concrete clad building, but inside there's a comfortable city tavern with separate rooms around a central bar. A favourite haunt of lawyers

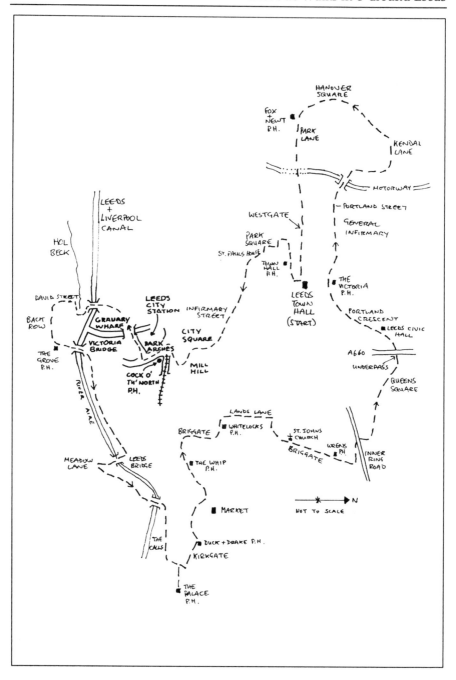

from the nearby law courts, there's Tetley Bitter, Mild, Imperial and Black Sheep bitter on tap.

Continue along The Headrow, to go through the first opening on the left into Park Square, whose elegant dwellings, now mainly offices, date from the late 18th and early 19th century. Turn left to the entrance into the gardens, and cross the Square with its statue of an elegant nymph pursued by three attendant wild boars. Directly ahead is one of Leeds's most splendid industrial buildings – St. Paul's House, originally a clothing factory, designed in 1878 in richly decorated Moorish style, with corner minarets, by Thomas Ambler, for Leeds entrepreneur John Barran.

Turn left out of the square into and along St. Paul's Street, crossing busy East Parade at the pedestrian crossing and walking along Infirmary Street, its name taken from the first Leeds Infirmary at this site, but now dominated by the fine baronial Yorkshire Penny Bank – now the Yorkshire Bank – building. Keep ahead into City Square, crossing Park Row, with the handsome renaissance-style Post Office on your right, built on the site of the old Coloured Cloth Hall, and in the Square, the equestrian statue of the Black Prince.

Turn right past Mill Hill Chapel, on the site of the old Presbyterian chapel one of whose ministers was Joseph Priestley, discoverer of oxygen, whose statue also stands in City Square.

Cross at the traffic lights and turn left into Boar Lane, going first right by the Griffin Inn down Mill Hill, its name a reference to the long vanished Kings Mill by the river which for centuries ground the town's corn .

Where Mill Hill meets Swinegate under the railway arches, on the left is the Prince of Wales tavern (see walk 7) but further left along the white lavatory tiles beyond the steps is the **Cock o'the North**, modestly describing itself as Britain's Ultimate Ale House, a relatively new pub skilfully built between Victorian railway arches which offers for a mainly young clientele at least a dozen real ales in a basic but atmospheric setting – including such delights as Black Sheep and Old Mill Bitter as well as ever changing guest beers.

Turn right to cross Bishopgate and head for the pedestrian lights to take you safely across Neville Street by the rear entrance to City Station. Turn left under the railway arches to the entrance to Granary Wharf – Leeds Dark Arches, an amazing shopping and flea market area by Leeds Canal Basin, and situated under the immense brick arches of the railway where the River Aire, Aire-Calder Navigation and the Leeds-Liverpool Canal meet.

Walk through this remarkable emporium to the opening on the left where you enter the Canal Basin. Make your way to the right across paved areas and past the crane, to cross the bridge over the Leeds Liverpool Canal and past the old Canal Offices and car park and new complex of warehouse-style offices to cross Holbeck into Wharf Lane. Turn right along Water Lane, and first left along David Street by the Matthew Murray building, noting Marshall's Mill Egyptian Temple on the right (see walk 2), turning first left past the car park into Back Row, a cul de sac at the end of which is **The Grove**, a traditional Victorian city pub which has been rescued from developers. The Grove has comfortable side rooms leading from the central bar, a stained glass illustration of barges on the canal, regular jazz on folk nights and hand-pulled John Smith's Bitter and Magnet, Director's and Bass.

Go to the end of Back Row and turn left along Victoria Road, crossing Water Lane at the lights and Victoria Bridge from where there are impressive views into Leeds Canal Basin, the great Leeds Liverpool Canal Warehouse of 1770, now a clothes shop, a dominant feature. Cross at the lights just below the KPMG building opposite. Turn right back to Victoria Bridge but take the steps through the ornamental metal gate past the KPMG buildings which lead to the riverside, following the elegantly designed walkway with terraces, benches, steps and lamps, passing Yorkshire Water Headquarters and car parks to emerge at Leeds Bridge. Turn right over Leeds Bridge to the **Old Red Lion** - a stage coach era tavern (Sam Smiths) built in 1809 with its original tavern sign and traditional bar, with excellent Sam Smith's Old Brewery Bitter available.

From the Old Red Lion cross at the pedestrian lights to the Adelphi (see Walk 3) before going past the Aire and Calder Navigation Offices (now British Waterways Board), along Dock Street, and bearing first left down Navigation Walk. Keep right along the granite cobbles past the new maisonettes skilfully converted from old warehouse buildings, past pool, fountains and footbridge, heading to Tetley's Brewery Wharf and the Centenary Bridge across the River Aire.

Cross here, turning right for 80 metres to where a narrow path cuts across the graveyard and past Leeds Parish Church. There has almost certainly been a church on this site since Saxon times, but the present neo-Gothic church dates from 1838.

It might be worth turning right beyond the church to **The Palace Hotel,** a Tetley's "Festival" Melbourne Inn on the site of an 18th century house and inn, the name recalling one of Leeds' lost breweries. There are usually at least 12 real ales available.

Cross Kirkgate and turn left into Church Lane, and right along the Church Walkway and Gardens, re-emerging on Kirkgate. Keep ahead along Kirkgate under the railway bridge immediately beyond which is the **Duck and Drake,** one of Leeds most popular real ale houses, a mecca for beer enthusiasts with at least a dozen classic real ales on offer, and usually stout and porters as well. Jazz on some evenings.

Cross Kirkgate to the opening beneath an archway almost directly opposite the Duck and Drake known as Pine Court leading under the brick railway arch Turn right in the pleasant brick-covered courtyard, to go right again under the next railway arch. This leads directly past the old Georgian Assembly Rooms. Ahead is the massive gritstone Corn Exchange, one of Leeds' grandest buildings and perhaps one of the finest mid-Victorian public buildings in the whole of Britain, designed by Leeds Town hall architect Cuthbert Brodrick. It's worth going inside to admire the magnificently engineered interior including the oval roof. Still used for the buying and selling of corn, it is also a busy shopping and market area, with rows of speciality shops on the two floors and around the balcony. On the way out, be sure to note the splendid Flemish-Venetian Leeds Market on the right along Vicar Lane, again one of the finest market halls in Britain with a richly decorated, highly colourful interior, full of wrought iron, and well worth seeing if you've time as well as being an excellent, bustling market.

Otherwise, go left at the Corn Exchange, turning left past the recently restored fragment of the historic White Cloth Hall down Call Lane, crossing at the lights, but taking the first opening right into Hurst's Yard, a typical Leeds medieval narrow courtyard or alleyway, half way along which you'll find **The Whip**, another classic Victorian Tetley's pub with a long bar, elongated to fit into the court with the usual Tetley Bitter, Mild and Imperial available but also an intriguing Tetley's Huntsman poster on the wall dating from the 1950s and boasting Mild at 1/2d and Bitter at 1/6p.

Hurst's Yard leads into Briggate directly opposite John Dyson's astonishingly decorated jeweller's shop. It's worth going back down

Briggate towards the railway to look into Lambert's Yard, another courtyard which boasts Leeds oldest surviving timber frame building or Queen's Court with its remarkable 18th century merchant's town house – now a smart restaurant.

Return to the Boar Lane traffic lights and walk up Briggate past Marks and Spencers' to where, in a ginnel just behind the Northern Rock Building Society, you'll find **Whitelocks,** originally known as The Turk's Head, and perhaps Leeds' most famous pub and "first luncheon bar". It may

Whitelocks

not look much from the outside, with clientele usually spilling onto the pavement and benches, but inside its long high copper covered bar and mirrors, frosted glass, twirling brass and period advertisements as well as cosy eating areas make this a living piece of Leeds history. The beer is extremely well-kept hand-pulled Younger's IPA., Scotch Bitter, No 3 and McEwan's 80/-, but the food of the old fashioned English variety is wholesome and delicious – but be warned it's always busy.

From Whitelocks continue along Turk's Head Yard into pedestrianised Lands Lane. Leeds was one of the first cities in Britain to develop extensive pedestrianisation of its central areas, and the restoration of the mainly Victorian and Edwardian shop and office frontages, giving the area a modern feel with contemporary street furniture and lighting.

Turn right up Lands Lane, noting another opening on the right, this time leading down to The Packhorse, site of an ancient inn now entirely rebuilt, across Bond Street junction and ahead to the top end of Land's Lane, past the Ship Inn ginnel and Queen's Arcade. Perhaps then turning into Thornton's Arcade, notable for the animated clock figurines of Robin Hood, Friar Tuck and Richard Lionheart, as you pass under the arch. This leads back into Briggate. Almost directly ahead on the opposite side is County Arcade, perhaps the most richly decorated of the Leeds arcades. Turn left past the entrance to the celebrated City Varieties music hall, occupying yet another alleyway, to the Headrow traffic lights. Cross into New Briggate, soon passing the entrance to St. John's Church on the left, one of Leeds' finest churches, unusual because it was built in the Civil War-torn 17th century, and Leeds Grand Theatre on the right, home of Opera North, and though unprepossessing on the outside, inside is one of England's most splendid theatres, a symphony of gilt and red plush.

Cross the traffic lights to **Wrens**, another classic Tetley's pub – this one is notable for being the Leeds theatrical pub, with a room decorated with photographs and memorabilia linked with actors, singers and performers at the nearby Grand.

From Wrens, take the road which slopes to the right of the pub

Passing The Wrens: the Tetley horses are regular entrants in the Lord Mayor's parade
(By kind permission of Joshua Tetley & Son)

past shops, keeping ahead on a narrow path through a small garden area above the Inner Ring Road in its deep cutting, following the pathway past a large post modern buildings which turns out to be the new Yorkshire Bank building on Wade Lane. Cross and turn right, heading for the Londoner pub. Turn left by the side of the Londoner along rough ground which leads into a pedestrian way between large concrete buildings – head for the Yorkshire Bank sign, by the steps of the Leeds Metropolitan University buildings. This emerges by a pedestrian crossing in Clay Pit lane.

Cross, turning left and then through the opening into Queen's Square, walking along the edge of a delightful early 19th century enclosed square of period terraced houses and offices with its central garden. The Square is still lit by gas, perhaps the last square in Leeds, if not in England, to be lit by traditional gas mantles.

The pub on the corner of Clay Pit Lane used to be a classic

Victorian pub with the resonant name The Coburg, recalling Prince Albert's home town in Franconia, northern Bavaria, but sadly has been sanitised into Scruffy Murphy's, a patronising attempt at Irishness, though its original name survives carved in the stonework. Ahead is a rather grim underpass, a typical '60s concrete people-sewer, which is nevertheless better than crossing the road. Go under, heading to the right for the Universities and Civic Hall. This emerges at Portland Street. Follow this down past the gleaming white portland stone of the Civic Hall, its twin towers topped by gilded owls, symbols of the city, noting the Civic Theatre, the former Mechanics Institute on the left, another Brodrick masterpiece.

Cross Calverley Street at the traffic lights, and turn right along George Street, behind the Town Hall. On the right is **The Victoria**, another celebrated Leeds tavern, with a richly gloomy, salon-like interior, boasting plush leather seats, globe lamps on spirals of brass, a luncheon room under stained glass and a vast bar – and the usual top quality Tetley beers.

Follow George Street past Sir Giles Gilbert Scott's splendid Gothic Infirmary built between 1863-7, now part of Leeds General Infirmary, the city's main hospital. Florence Nightingale advised on the original design to maximise light and air for patients.

Continue along George Street past St. George's church and Crypt to where a pedestrian and cycle bridge crosses to Woodhouse Square – the bronze statue facing you being Sir Peter Fairbairn, Lord Mayor of Leeds 1857/8. Turn right into Clarendon Road past handsome Victorian houses, to Claremont, offices of Yorkshire Archaeological Society and the Thoresby Society and where, opposite Little Woodhouse Street, a cobbled lane leads between walls. This is Kendal Lane, reputedly a surviving fragment of the medieval packhorseway which was used by clothiers from Kendal and the higher Dales to reach Leeds Market on Briggate.

Follow Kendal Lane past a couple of corner shops to where, just before the pillar box, Hanover Square leads off to the left. Take this, passing Denison Hall, a grand neo-classical stone mansion built by Leeds merchant John Denison in 1786, but now sadly derelict.

Cross the little parkland Hanover Square to the bottom right-hand corner which leads into the bottom of Burley Road at Park Lane, where by the junction with Burley Street you'll see our last pub, the **Fox and Newt**, notable as being the only other brewery to Tetley's in Leeds. It's a micro-brewery on the premises which offers such delectation as Cushie's Bitter, their own stout with the evocative name of Diesel and perhaps most startling of all a light green beer known as Ghost-Buster, the name linked to odd activities in the old pub which is reputedly haunted. Very quaffable beers and a pleasant atmosphere.

From the Fox and Newt cross at the pedestrian lights by Park Lane College, and walk back into the city centre, keeping slightly to the right at the Ring Road interchange, to cross, at the pedestrian lights into Westgate, with the great baroque tower of the Town Hall directly ahead.

Leeds Town Hall

Walk 2: Middleton Woods, Hunslet Moor and Holbeck

A walk rich in history, past one of the world's first fully incorporated railways, through surviving areas of open common to the workshops and warehouses where Leeds first began to develop into a great manufacturing city.

Distance: 7km (4 mls)

Maps: Landranger 104; Pathfinders 683, 692

Start: Middleton Arms, Middleton

Finish: Leeds City Square

Getting there: Take any (frequent) bus from the Corn Exchange to Middleton Arms – e.g. 10, 20, 22, 24, 35 plus other services. Motorists should park in the city centre, take the bus and walk back to their car.

The Pub

The Gardeners Arms, Hunslet (0113 271 2971). A real gem – a delightful traditional Victorian pub, squeezed in between two industrial buildings, and opposite a surviving fragment of Hunslet Moor, once an ancient area of open common, now a recreational ground. Old fashioned bar, comfortable snugs, beer garden at the back and open fire. Tetley's Bitter as it should be served. Sandwiches and bar snacks usually available. All day opening.

The Walk

From the Middleton Arms bus stops, cross Middleton Park Road and Circus to the Middleton Arms – a large, typical 1930s pub – and

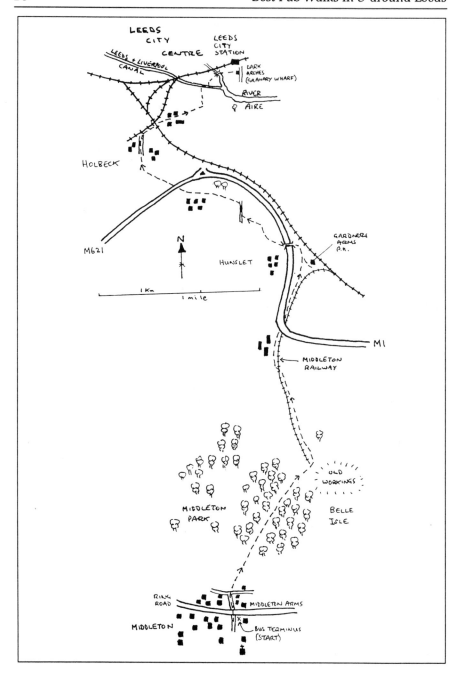

continue along St. Philips Road directly past the pub to its junction with Town Street and the entrance to Middleton Park opposite.

Middleton Park is one of Leeds' largest parks, with an extensive area of woodland, a golf course, tennis courts, playing fields and numerous walks. There are wide-ranging views from the park's elevated position across the great bowl of the Aire valley and the tower blocks and spires of Leeds city centre. Until the late 1950s it also had an important footnote in urban transport history, carrying the Middleton Light Railway, a part of Leeds' extensive tramway system on its own separate reservation around the edge of the Park, built to link this extensive suburb with the city centre. Its abandonment in favour of slower, traffic congested buses was a seriously retrograde step.

Turn sharp right along the main park drive, past shrubbery, tennis courts, a pool for model boats, toilets and a pleasant cafe at the top of the woods. Continue into the less formal area of Middleton Woods – a delightful and extensive area of semi-natural woodland pitted with old mine workings dating from the 18th century.

The track eventually emerges from the wood – keep straight ahead to a junction of tracks, bearing right past old mine workings and the young trees of the new Belle Isle Wood (on the site of the old Belle Isle mining village) to reach the southern terminus of the Middleton Railway.

Though this little preserved line is barely half a mile long, it has a secure place in history, dating back to 1758 when Charles Brandling, a local coal owner, obtained Parliamentary approval to operate a railway line from his collieries nearby to carry coal down to wharfs on the River Aire, at that time recently improved into the Aire and Calder Navigation, for export by river and coastal shipping. The railway which now occupies the site of part of this historic line is now operated by the Middleton Railway Trust on summer weekends with a variety of vintage steam and diesel locomotives.

Paths in the area are subject to change (the right of way on most OS maps has been diverted around the new sports stadium), but there are well-used permissive routes on each side of the old railway.

The pleasanter route is the grassy path to the left about 15 metres past the railway which goes through young woods along the right-hand side of the line. Immediately past the stadium, look for an informal gap in the hedge and crossing of the railway, then follow the path at the side of the railway, soon bearing left to a more obvious path parallel to the railway. This leads over a grassy mound. Where the railway divides right through a tunnel and left into a scrap merchants, follow the left branch to cross a little level crossing to a tunnel under the M1. Keep ahead to rejoin the line, keeping between railway and motorway to the terminus station of the Middleton Railway. If you are doing the walk on a summer weekend, check departure times for a ride and visit to the railway – a small shop and museum are open at other times for visitors.

Otherwise keep straight ahead along the tarmac path which goes through and underneath a concrete clover-leaf junction past not unattractive central gardens. Keeping the same direction towards the playing field ahead which is a surviving piece of Hunslet Moor – on the right, surrounded on three sides by a large engineering works, you'll see the remarkable little Gardeners Arms.

On leaving the pub, head over the Moor to the railway line and prominent footbridge over the M1 towards another remnant of Hunslet Moor on the other side. Turn right at the far side of the motorway and walk across pleasant open grass, protected from some of the traffic noise by high grassy mounds to the left.

Keep ahead by the Blooming Rose pub and a children's playground, heading for Moor Road and the two massive cerise and cream blocks of flats ahead – Crescent Grange and Crescent Towers, to The Junction pub on Dewsbury Road. Cross at the lights, and turn right past modern houses at Northcote Court, to where a tarmac path branches off over the grass. Ignore this, turning sharp left along the path which goes along the back of gardens beyond Northcote Crescent, along the edge of the recreation ground. Keep ahead past tennis courts towards a white building which is the Old Golden Lion Hotel ahead on the now truncated Beeston Road, to the left of which a broad underpass goes underneath the M621 Leeds urban motorway.

Amazingly, this leads you to another attractive park and open space, the residual fragment of another ancient common, Holbeck Moor. Keep ahead past gardens, but cross to the black outline of St. Matthew's Church, now a community centre, behind which, in the landscaped graveyard, now an open space, you'll see the massive monument to one of Leeds' most famous engineers, Matthew Murray, who with John Blenkinsop developed highly efficient rack-driven steam locomotives, precursors of Stephenson's more famous Rocket. In 1812 – 14 years before the Stockton and Darlington Railway opened – the Salamanca and Prince Regent astonished observers by hauling a train of 38 loaded waggons at 3 mph across Hunslet Moor.

Bear right, and cross Stocks Hill directly ahead and into Bridge Street, heading past the celebrated Holbeck Engine Sheds towards the garage, Bristol Street Motors, just before which, just past the junction with Sweet Street, a narrow and highly atmospheric ginnel leads between blue brick lavatory tile walls under tall narrow arches carrying the railway line. Keep ahead into waste ground, usually

Marshall's Mill

occupied by gypsies and scrap car merchants, over the remnants of Bath Road (a reminder that Holbeck was once a small spa). Follow the continuation of the ginnel which emerges at the remarkable Marshall's Mill, a flax mill designed like a vast mock Egyptian Temple, built 1838-40 to the design of Igantius Bonomi and based on a temple at Edfu. It is reputed that during war time a flock of sheep once grazed on its grass-covered flat roof.

Follow the continuation of the ginnel past new office buildings into David Street, turning left to Water Street, emerging at the site of Matthew Murray's old foundry and, a whole complex of early Industrial Revolution workshops and courtyards where Leeds first developed as a major manufacturing city. Cross the road – the stream running in the culvert is the actual Hol Beck, its Saxon name similar to such names of streams as you'll find in Germany, and doubtless dating back to the earliest settlements in the city. Turn right for a few metres to the entrance to Granary Wharf, turning left past the car parks, then right past the Old Canal offices and bridge over the Canal leading into the dark arches and city centre.

Walk 3: Thwaite Mills

The Aire & Calder Navigation, Leeds' oldest and still most important waterway, provides a green corridor of waterway and embankment into the centre of Leeds. This walk along its towpath gives insight into the city's historic role as an inland port, passing, at Thwaite Mills, a living link with the early years of the Industrial Revolution.

Distance: 10km (6½ mls)

Maps: Landranger 104; Pathfinders 683, 692

Start: Woodlesford Station (Hallam or Pontefract Line)

Finish: Briggate, Leeds

Getting there: Frequent train services to Woodlesford from Leeds. Motorists should park in Leeds and catch the train; alternatively park in Woodlesford (free car park) and return by train from Leeds at the end of the walk.

The Pub

The Garden Gate, Hunslet (0113 270 0379) is well worth the short deviation from the main route. A justly celebrated Tetley's Heritage pub, its fine brick and tile exterior (see cover) is nothing compared with an interior which is a riot of Victorian frosted glass and oak woodwork, with an ornate art nouveau green tiled central bar, old fashioned side rooms serviced from the hatch and coal fires. This pub is an unspoiled gem, a piece of old Hunslet surviving in an area transformed by new motorways, warehousing, housing developments and shopping centres. Outstandingly fine Tetley Bitter available – but note that children are not admitted in this very traditional pub.

The Adelphi

The Adelphi, Leeds Bridge (01132 456377) is one of the most famous and best known pubs in Leeds. A fine, four storey late Victorian beer palace (built 1900), clad in polished granite and red brick, it is richly decorated inside in dark mahogany and cut and frosted glass, with a central bar and comfortably furnished side rooms or snugs, popular for meetings. Jazz at weekends. Another of Tetley's Heritage Pubs, and the unofficial Tetley's Tap, (though owned originally by the Melbourne brewery), it has been carefully restored to its former splendours. Tetley Bitter, Mild and Imperial are as good as you'll get anywhere in the city – and the ideal terminus for a nine kilometre walk.

The Walk

From Woodlesford Station, cross the little car park and bear right along the path which leads into Station Lane. Keep ahead with the tarmac path by the green and towards the church spire, keeping right at the fork. This leads into Pottery Lane. Cross to the footpath and turn right here, following the lane downhill and curving right to where, on the left, an opening leads to Woodlesford Lock on the Aire and Calder Navigation, an attractive grassy area usually busy with leisure craft. Cross the stile by the lock keeper's house, and cross the footbridge over the canal locks. Turn left along the tow-path.

This section of the Navigation – the Knostrop Cut – has the River Aire and the 18th century canalised section running parallel, with the path following the narrow strip of land that separates the two, the river meandering below, at first close and then curving away from the river. You are soon looking across a series of artificial lakes or flashes produced in the valley floor by mining subsistence. This is a well-worked landscape, with traces of industrial activity, mostly restored and renatured, evident on all sides, and evidence of straightening of various sections of river even before the Knostrop Cut was put in during the 1770s. It's also a fine area for birdlife, with moorhen, swan, coot, sandmartin usually evident on the river edges or around the reedbeds. There are fine views across Lower Airedale to Temple Newsam estate, with if the weather is clear, Temple Newsam House just visible close to the woods on the horizon.

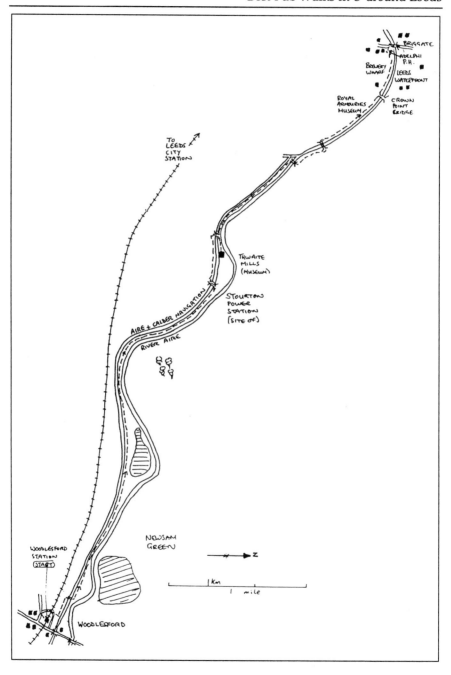

The path continues past Fishpond Lock and, after a little under three kilometres – less than 2 miles – you reach a concrete bridge carrying the trackbed of an old railway line. The path forks. Keep to the new section of path along the riverside, under the bridge.

River and Navigation curve northwards, soon passing the site of the former Skelton Power Station on the right, along an attractive treelined section of canal. Keep ahead between river and canal to where the path ascends steps to a metal gate and bridge. Cross the bridge to the far side of the canal, going left down steps and back underneath the bridge to join the path along the canal, soon passing Thwaite Mills on the far side of the canal. Reach the main drive into Thwaite Mills, then turn right into the mills complex.

In 1823-4 a new water-powered mill was built here along the Aire and Calder Navigation to replace a 17th century fulling mill. Its purpose was to crush linseed imported via the waterway for lighting and machinery lubrication; it is said that oil from Thwaite Mills was used to lubricate Stephenson's Rocket. In 1872 the mills were adapted to grind flint and china stone for use by the local pottery industry, as well as barytes for paint and especially chalk for whitewash, putty making, polish, chemicals – and even in food. By the mid 20th century only putty was produced here, a manufacturing process which continued until 1976 when a flood damaged the weir, forcing the mill to close. It was restored between that time and 1990 by the Thwaite Mills Society, and the Mills now form a unique industrial museum with water-wheels, engineering workshop, a water-powered crane and a former mill manager's house, with presentations, exhibitions and some refreshments available. There are regular guided tours. The Mills are open daily except Mondays.

From Thwaite Mills, take the path directly opposite the main complex and which continues along an elevated section of tow-path past the remains of Hunslet Railway Bridge, a former rail freight line, and the weir, soon reaching Knostrop Lock. Keep ahead along a long straight section for some 700 metres to Knostrop Flood Lock.

For the Garden Gate Inn, take the wooden footbridge on the left which leads over the canalised section of river by the lock, and follow the path around the lock keeper's cottage and along an enclosed way past an arm of the canal which forms a dock. This path emerges into an industrial estate road. Turn right and head for the traffic island, keeping straight ahead along Old Mill Lane, past car showrooms to the Wellington pub by traffic lights on Low Road – the busy A61. Cross at the pedestrian lights turning right to cross Church Lane, going left for 50 metres then first right along Whitfield Way, left along Whitfield Avenue and right again along Whitfield Place – the tall brick building ahead is the Garden Gate.

Return the same way to Knostrop Lock, but this time take the narrow footbridge to the right that crosses the River Aire and follows the narrow riverside path between fences which goes past industrial plant and then the modern office development, emerging at South Accommodation Bridge. Cross the bridge, going down the steps on the left at the far side, back down to the tow-path on the western bank, and back under South Accommodation Road.

Continue along the path through a great brick and stone canyon formed by high factory walls, with intriguing views of St Savior's Church glimpsed between factories and foundries across the river, soon passing Leeds Lock, the only manually operated lock between Leeds and the sea.

You soon reach the new Leeds Armouries. The path skirts this newest of Museums, by Clarence Dock, before dipping down by Leeds Dam to go underneath Crown Point Bridge and into the Leeds Basin. On the right are the converted warehouses along the Calls which now form the city's newest and most fashionable city centre apartments, on the left Brewery Wharf, Tetley's Museum of Brewing. Don't cross Centenary Bridge but keep ahead along the path which leads past an ornamental dock-like pool, complete with fountains, fashionable maisonettes, and cobblestones, and into Navigation Walk. Turn left at the end and then right into Dock Street which leads to the end of Leeds Bridge and the Adelphi.

From the Adelphi it is a short walk across Leeds Bridge and along Briggate to the city centre.

Walk 4: Gledhow Woods And Buslingthorpe

The first part of this walk explores a surviving section of a wooded Pennine valley squeezed between the semi-detacheds of suburban Leeds. This is a route popular with ramblers of many generations, but the return via the Meanwood Valley to the city centre is far less well known, using a network of paths via the old settlement of Buslingthorpe that reaches almost to the heart of the city.

Distance: 6.5km (4 mls)

Maps: Landranger 104; Pathfinder 683

Start: Astoria, Roundhay Road

Finish: City Centre

Getting there: Any bus service to the Astoria on Roundhay Road (one stop past Fforde Green traffic lights at Harehills). Frequent buses e.g. 10, 19, 21 from Briggate, 98 from Infirmary Street. Motorists should park in Leeds and take the bus.

The Pubs

The Nag's Head, Chapel Allerton (0113 262 4938) is a pub dating back to the 17th century, in a quiet yard on Chapel Allerton's old Town Street, going back to the days when Chapel Allerton was an outlying village just off the main Harrogate turnpike road. White walls, low beams and frothy pints of Sam Smith's Old Brewery Bitter. Food most times, friendly atmosphere.

    The Eagle Tavern, Sheepscar, (0113 245 7146) is a favourite amongst Leeds lovers of real ale. A tall, bow-windowed tavern dating back to Regency times and the more leisurely days of stage coaches, it now lies close to an expressway interchange out of the city – a hazard to be negotiated by walkers. The excellence of the ale makes car-dodging worth the effort, as befits Timothy Taylor's only major outlet in the city centre. Such delights as Ram Tam, Golden Best, Taylor's Dark Mild, regular Taylor's Bitter and Landlord on offer – and guest beers as well. Jazz on Sundays, but the pub does close promptly at 3pm, so time your visit carefully.

The Walk

Alight at the Astoria, once a popular dance hall and now a pub and club, with an electrical suppliers shop dominating the more obvious white roadside facade. Go round behind the building on its little island of roads, crossing to follow Gledhow Wood Road directly behind, passing typical between-the-wars semis. But after barely 250 metres the semis end and the road enters a steep, wooded valley.

Gledhow Woods

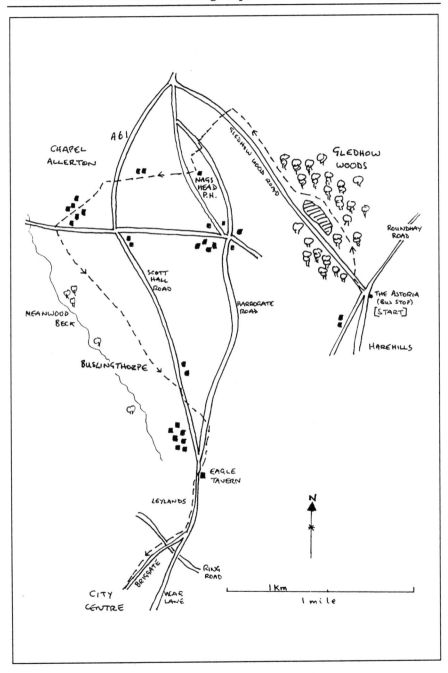

Just past the 40 mph sign, look for a narrow path, right, which leaves the tarmac roadside path and heads into the woods. Look sharp right and you will see, partially concealed by trees, a little stone building. This is Gipton Spa, a tiny cold water bathhouse dating from 1671 where the gouty and rheumatic once sought fairly drastic cold water cures – though water was also heated by a small fire for hot-and-cold treatments.

Take the narrow path which slopes up the woodland, away from the road with its fast moving traffic and into a surprisingly fine relic woodland with oak, birch and beech trees hanging to the steep slope. As houses come into view ahead, look for a narrow path which forks left, leading up to a path which slopes gently back down towards the roadside, with fine views all the way. This path goes parallel with the road before reaching a little ornamental pond. Follow the path around the outside of the pond, continuing beyond to where there are stone entrance gates. Ignore these, either follow the streamside or the higher path on the right, the latter with perhaps better views. Keep ahead, ignoring sleeper steps on the right, to where Gledhow Lane, a wide crossing road, cuts across the valley. The path continues upstream behind the Leisure Services "No tipping" notice, but is now very much narrower and goes through damp undergrowth of willowherb and shrubs, the surface a little muddy, following the beck, past culverts, winding over a tarmac crossing path. Where an open grassy recreation area comes into view, and the stream swings right alongside a concrete path, take this path left to the main road.

Turn right for around 25 metres and cross to where, directly opposite, you should see stone steps and a handrail. This leads to a path by a sloping area of grass and into Pasture Lane. It is pleasant to keep on the grass, parallel to Pasture Lane to a tarmac path which leads into a park. Keep in the same direction past the park tennis courts, the path swinging back left into Pasture Lane. Go left into Woodland Lane, then turn right at the junction into Regent Street past the Regent pub (Tetley's), taking Hawthorn Road on the left. This leads into Town Street where straight ahead, by the Methodist Chapel, you'll see the Nag's Head, set back from the street.

From the Nag's Head turn left back along Town Street, into Chapel Allerton village and Harrogate Road. Cross at the pedestrian crossing, then turn left into Stainbeck Lane, an extremely old lane which crosses the hills of north Leeds, its Anglo-Saxon name denoting the "stony beck" which still trickles down a largely built up hillside close by.

Even suburbanisation has not entirely destroyed its character, and there are open views over the playing fields as you approach Scott Hall Road. Cross this busy dual carriageway at the pedestrian lights, continuing for about 70 metres along Stainbeck Lane past the traffic island, before turning left into Stainbeck Walk, along what appears to be a cul de sac. Keep ahead at the end, going along what appears to be a grassy drive to a garage, but which is in fact an entrance to a quite remarkable and largely secret Leeds ginnel, a long straight path between gardens, lit by tall lamps (though I suspect few people venture along it after dark).

Stainbeck Walk emerges into Miles Hill Road where you should cross directly along the path's continuation which in fact leads down a slope into the car park of the Hill Top Pub. Walk through the car park, to a tarmac path by the playground which leads down to Potternewton Road. Cross again, this time to a wooden gap stile just to the right. This leads into a path to two further gap stiles. Ignore the obvious one ahead which leads down into the Meanwood Valley, but take the stile on the left. Once through here, turn sharp left to follow the fence and hedge along the top of a sloping field towards a step stile in the corner of the field. Below you is the Leeds Urban Farm, an amazing rural survivor which until recently was a working farm, but remains viable as a remarkable conservation and education project where Leeds children can see a variety of domestic animals in an authentic farm setting.

The path now goes along a narrow enclosure between hedges and fences. At another stile leading back into Potternewton Road, take the path right which follows the top of the slope, now with quite superb views along the entire Meanwood Valley and into the city centre, (see Walk 5) a remarkable juxtaposition of woodland and industry, with the Parkinson Tower of Leeds University, church towers and tower blocks of the city centre forming an impressive backcloth.

A little radio mast now forms a useful waymark. Follow the track past it, heading to and past the rugby field, at the far right hard corner of which you'll find steps which take the path snaking down the hillside until you eventually reach a crossroads. Turn left along a narrow cobbled way towards the mill chimney in Buslingthorpe Vale.

Buslingthorpe was once a small settlement north of Leeds, which in the Industrial Revolution became a heaving tangle of activity – a complex of mills, workshops, tenements, forges and tanners' yards along Sheepscar Beck. The fine early Industrial Revolution mill just survives in a ruinous state as does Buslingthorpe Lane, cut through by Scott Hall Road, a "relief" road built in the 1930s.

Sadly the last kilometre of this walk is a savage indictment of what the private car and its acolytes, the road traffic engineers, have done to our urban environment – with huge radial highways and high speed traffic obliterating what remains of both Buslingthorpe and Sheepscar. The pub however really is worth it – and the worst is soon passed.

Follow Buslingthorpe Lane left to its junction with Scott Hall Road. Cross at the pedestrian lights, and continue along the rump of Buslingthorpe Lane. This leads into Sheepscar Way, a cul-de-sac of neat little offices surrounded by lawns. Walk straight ahead up the grassy slope and make for the pedestrian lights directly ahead which lead (safely) across the multi-lane urban motorway that in more civilised times used to be the bottom of Chapeltown Road. Cross, turning right past the Ramgarha Sikh Centre and the West Yorkshire County Archive at Sheepscar. Cross Roundhay Road ahead. At the next pedestrian lights, just before the Pointer pub, cross back to the right over the triple carriageway again, this time turning into the remnants of North Street – a few lonely former shops and a derelict garage looking stranded on what has become a blighted island between the expressways.

Things improve after this point, because just beyond the next crossing along North Street is that mecca for ramblers and ale lovers, The Eagle Tavern.

From The Eagle cross the four-lane speedway (at the lights), and walk towards the city along the grassy verge of North Street. But soon past the first junction on the right take the steps, right, which lead to a narrow path above, screened from traffic by shrubs, alongside gardens – follow this to and across Grafton Street, keeping the same direction across the grass into and around the edge of a small park, The Leylands. At the end of the park keep ahead along North Street past the slip road to the Inner Ring Road, crossing at a higher level (at least the traffic is below you). Ahead is New Briggate and the city centre.

```
┌─────────────────────────────────────────────────────────┐
│ ┌─────────────────────────────────────────────────────┐ │
│ │                                                       │ │
│ │    Walk 5: The Meanwood Valley and                    │ │
│ │    The Hollies                                        │ │
│ │                                                       │ │
│ └─────────────────────────────────────────────────────┘ │
└─────────────────────────────────────────────────────────┘
```

*An ideal short walk for a winter afternoon or summer evening
– from Woodhouse Moor along a series of linking ginnels
through the historic Meanwood Valley to Meanwood Park
and Woods and the remarkable Hollies, two of Leeds' most
attractive and distinctive parks.*

Distance: 7km (4 mls)

Maps: Landranger 104; Pathfinder 683

Start: Woodhouse Moor (Hyde Park Corner)

Finish: West Park

Getting there: Buses 1A, 93, 94, 95, 96 (frequent) from Leeds Infirmary
Street or 1, 28 from Briggate to Hyde Park Corner – or walk (1 mile) from
City Centre via Woodhouse Lane, Leeds University and Woodhouse
Moor. Motorists: park at Woodhouse Moor and return to start by equally
frequent direct bus.

The Pub

The Myrtle Tavern, Parkside Road, Meanwood (0113 275 2101).
Popular pub which has developed from a typical rural tavern in a
row of mill cottages on the edge of the city. Despite extensions to
the original terrace that forms the pub, it retains a remarkable rural
feeling, opposite Meanwood Cricket ground, despite being close to
the densely populated suburbs of Meanwood. Open all day, welcoming to walkers with a pleasant ambience, food and bar snacks
at lunchtime, coffee; John Smiths and Magnet from the cask.

The Walk

From Hyde Park Corner bus stop and traffic lights (and the northern end of Woodhouse Moor, an ancient common), cross to the Hyde Park pub and turn right down Woodhouse Street, going left opposite the post office along Cliff Road. Past the Cliff Centre, turning left again at the next corner along Cross Cliff Road, past attractive cottages then right into Cliff Lane, past more Victorian terraces and gardens.

After 100 metres just past Grove Park Gardens (apartments) on the left, look for a narrow ginnel on the left which runs between stone walls and fences of gardens. Follow this past a crossing road, keeping the same direction into Grosvenor Road by a bench and small area of green. Cross the road and turn right for a few metres to locate the continuation of the ginnel between high stone walls, emerging by Devonshire Hall in Cumberland Road. Steer right to yet a further extension of the ginnel which leads from the end of Cumberland Road into Woodhouse Ridge, a park formed of the steep valley sides of the Meanwood Valley. Turn left, but where the path forks, bear right down a series of concrete steps, with long views along this quite remarkable piece of countryside so close to Leeds city centre. There are open views across the valley to the right where you can see cows and horses grazing in inner Leeds in what is now the Meanwood Urban Farm (see Walk 4). The valley bottom itself, lined with the remains of old water mills is rich in industrial archaeology, a complex blend of rural and urban.

Follow the path as it leads straight ahead over a footbridge across the Meanwood Beck and scruffy remains of industrial buildings to reach Grove Lane. Cross carefully, and turn left for 200 metres to where you'll cross Meanwood Beck again and pick up the Meanwood Valley Trail – marked by a Leeds owl – along a narrow path between the beck and gardens of tall terraced houses.

Keep ahead to Monk Bridge Road. Cross and follow Highbury Lane towards the tall black mill chimney ahead, following a path to a fine but sadly derelict mill. Turn left along a cobbled path past the mill pond, then right through the allotment and past a bowling green

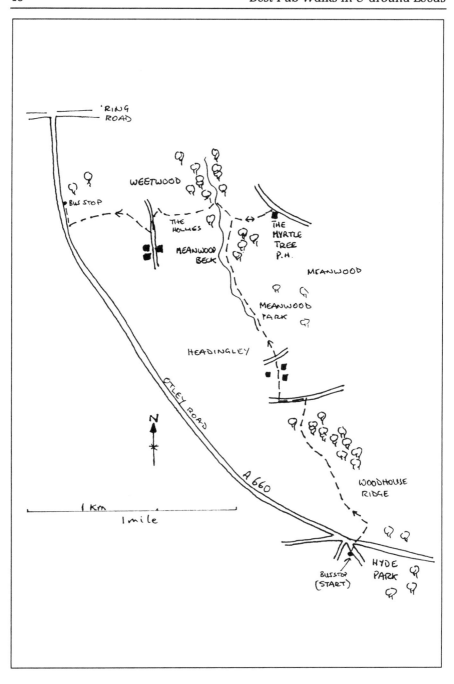

and cricket pitch. As the path approaches a suburban road ahead, take the path sharp right over a footbridge, between beck and cricket pitch, but after 60 metres go through a gap stile in the stone wall left which leads into Meanwood Park.

This beautiful park once was the country estate of the Kitson family, famous engineers and locomotive builders, a now sadly departed Leeds industry.

You pass a small picnic area. Cross the grass, then keeping roughly alongside the stream to your left, walk up the valley. This eventually leads to a stile into a crossing path by a footbridge, opposite a long row of mill cottages, Hustlers Lane, built to serve a long vanished Weetwood Mill, whose mill race remains. At Hustlers Row turn right along the lane past the end of the cottages, but enter the oak woods behind the grassy area to your right, and follow the path which climbs steeply up a rocky hillside and through the oakwoods, remarkable relics of ancient Pennine woods. At the top of the hill, follow the path as it bears left around the edge of the field by the hedge and fence which forms the boundary of the woods. Look carefully for a narrow opening on the right, just before you reach a line of extended fence on the bluff ahead. From here a distinct path passes a small sandstone quarry face and follows the field, soon turning right (now a public right of way) to emerge at a cottage ahead by the Meanwood cricket pitch. Turn left here for the Myrtle Tavern.

From the inn, retrace your steps back to the old quarry and into Meanwood Woods. This time descend the hillside – there are lines of path – down to the mill-race crossed by a footbridge and into The Hollies.

The Hollies, the hillside gardens of a former country house which is now an old peoples' residential home, forms spectacular rhodo-dendron and azaleas gardens, never more splendid than in late May or early June when the hillside blazes with colour, and with tall primula candelabra in every nook and sike.

A huge choice of ways through the park, but you need to make your way carefully uphill by a choice of zigzagging ways until you reach the tennis courts. Turn left along the path below the courts, but take the first rocky steps right which emerge at a tall beech hedge below the Hollies house.

Turn left here, to an exquisite sheltered garden of lawns, herbaceous borders and magnolia. Keep ahead to the entrance (unless you wish to explore more of the park – if so turn right just by the entrance past the rockery to the philadelphus and hosta gardens) and pass the lodge into Weetwood Lane.

Left here for 30 metres, but cross opposite the school to the metal pedestrian guard opposite, behind which yet another lovely long ginnel enclosed between high stone walls leads to the drive into Oxley Hall. At the end of the ginnel take the steps in the wall opposite, and turn left by the playing fields to follow the path which leads to the busy Otley Road. Turn right to the bus stop for frequent buses back to Hyde Park Corner or the centre of Leeds.

Walk 6: Roundhay Park and Shadwell

Through one of the finest parks in the north of England and across Leeds' Green Belt to the still unspoiled village of Shadwell.

Distance: 7km (4½ mls)

Maps: Landranger 104; Pathfinder 683

Start and Finish (Circular): Roundhay Park – main entrance

Public Toilets: In Roundhay Park just to the north of the Mansion House.

Getting There: Buses 10, 19 from Briggate. Motorists park in large free car park by the rose gardens.

The Pub

The Red Lion, Shadwell (0113 273 7463). Popular Tetley's pub which has retained something of its local village pub atmosphere in spite of extensions for a restaurant. Tetley Bitter, Mild and Imperial; food available most times.

The Walk

Start at the main entrance to Roundhay Park, past the impressive wrought iron gates. This 700 acre park was acquired from the Nicholson family, wealthy London bankers, by the relatively young Borough of Leeds in 1872 after much public debate, and was served by one of the city's first tram services. The old and much lamented tram terminus by the rose garden is now the main car park – but the posts which carried the overhead wires remain as evocative symbols of Leeds' first Tram Age.

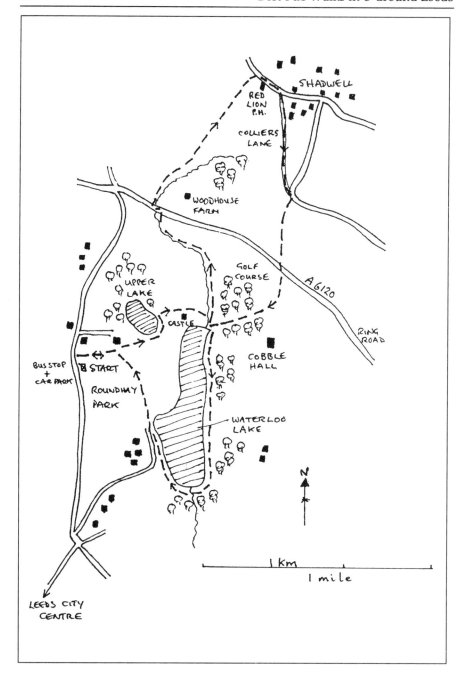

Roundhay Park has been developed over the years by the City Council into one of the most popular and delightful parks in Britain. Outstanding features include the lovely Canal Gardens and its hugely popular Tropical World glasshouse complex, the neo-classical Mansion House, designed by York architect John Carr and erected around 1820, the magnificent Waterloo Lake created in 1815, and the densely wooded valley that carries Great Heads Beck into the lake – to be explored on this walk. But if you haven't been to the Park before, you may wish to spend rather more time here than the walk allows. There is also a choice of refreshment facilities within the Park itself – at the Canal Gardens, Waterloo Lake or the Mansion House.

Continue along the main drive, past the Mansion House with its impressive colonnade. As the main track reaches a junction, walk directly ahead, over and down the grassy slope ahead, towards the little Upper Lake you will see below. Head for the lake to join the pathway to the right around the lake, soon crossing above a little wooded area where there is a waterfall and a little Victorian grotto.

Keep ahead past the end of the lake to where the path meets another crossing path. Turn right, parallel to the tracks of the Roundhay Park miniature railway – where the path forks, keep right (do not cross the miniature railway) descending past the mock ruins of a Castle, once known as the Ivy Castle, though the ivy has long been eradicated. It is in fact a 19th century folly, put there purely for picturesque effect, with its battlements offering fine views of Waterloo Lake below.

Follow the main path down into a shallow valley, in dense woodland; until you reach a stone bridge. Turn left here on what starts as a narrow path but soon becomes a broader path through lovely oak woods, going upstream above the Great Heads Beck, and crossing no less than 13 wooded plank bridges until, at the head of the valley, the path ascends to a fine, tall arched stone bridge. Cross the stile over the bridge and turn right up to the Leeds Ring Road.

Cross the Ring Road with extreme care (traffic travels at up to 70 mph) to pick up the continuation of the path, signed, at a pedestrian barrier. This becomes a lovely, partially surfaced path by tall hedgerows and a branch of the beck, passing fields before bearing right and then left, alongside tall hedges, going directly into Shadwell village.

Shadwell village has grown in recent years – and may grow again in the future as the city expands, but at the moment, protected by a strong, if threatened, Green Belt policy, keeps its rural charm, with a village post office and 19th century cottages. Turn right for about 50 metres to the Red Lion inn.

From the pub, continue in the same direction to Collier Lane, an estate road which, where the tarmac turns sharp left into Blind Lane, continues as a lovely bridleway between fields. As the countryside opens out, again you get the most spectacular views of the city spread out ahead of you – spires and tower blocks in the great bowl of the Aire Valley between the hills that contain the city.

Follow the path past another road end, keeping ahead along the bridleway till you reach the Ring Road once again. Again, cross with care, taking the continuation which is a grassy path across Leeds Golf Course. Go straight ahead, heeding the warning against flying golf balls, for about 250 metres to a strip of woodland ahead. Look for narrow steps on the right just past the remains of a gateway, in the wood, leading to a narrow path which again crosses another open stretch of golf course. Keep in the same direction dipping down towards the woods ahead. Once in the wood, take the clear path straight in front of you which descends to the edge of Waterloo Lake. Turn left along the lakeside path.

This magnificent boating lake in its lovely parkland setting is a kilometre long – three quarters of a mile, and about 20 metres deep in the centre. Follow the path to the dam and the southern end, crossing the dam with its fine views to the main park promenade. Turn right along the main drive past the boat-house cafe and bearing left at the little funfair, soon walking past the amphitheatre, site of many top Leeds sporting and entertainment events – including such international luminaries as Michael Jackson and the Rolling Stones.

The path ascends to the main drive. Keep left for the main entrance, bus stops and car park.

Walk 7: Kirkstall Abbey

This walk may only take a couple of hours, but it is worth giving yourself sufficient time not only to look around the Abbey itself, but to visit either Abbey House Museum or the Leeds Industrial Museum in Armley Mills as part of a day out – but remember they close on Mondays.

Distance: 8km (5 mls)

Maps: Landranger 104; Pathfinder 683

Start: Headingley Station

Finish: City Square

Public Toilets: Kirkstall Abbey

Getting there: Frequent rail service (MetroTrain Harrogate line) to Headingley. Motorists park in the city centre and take the train.

Kirkstall Abbey is perhaps the finest early Cistercian monastic ruin in the British Isles, attracting romantic poets and topographers alike. Though now surrounded on all sides by industry and suburbia, enough parkland and woodland survive to form a lovely green canal and railway corridor into the city, and to give an impression of what this part of Airedale was like when the Cistercians first cleared a settlement in the forest.

The Pub ·

The Prince of Wales in Swinegate (0113 245 2434)- at the end of the walk – is a popular and unpretentious city centre pub, with a touch of faded but comfortable Edwardiana, Toby jugs on the shelf, stone sherry barrel in the corner, and is rightly known for the excellence

of its ales – John Smiths Bitter, Directors and a guest beer – usually
Black Sheep. Juke box can be noisy on occasions, otherwise always
welcoming. Open all day.

The Walk

From Headingley Station (if coming from the Leeds direction) go
down the exit steps and turn right through the subway under the
railway line, and along the tarmac footpath between allotments to
Queenswood Drive. Cross, and make for the tarmac path to the left
of the flats in Queenswood Rise towards the trees ahead. Where the
path turns sharp right into housing, keep ahead soon bearing uphill
on a narrow path into Batcliffe Wood, heading between trees for the
path ahead which runs along a low ridge. Turn left here and follow
the path by mature beech trees until the path opens out into the
expanse of Beckett's Park. Follow the broad open grassy way past
the Middle School on the left, but turn left, with the college ahead,
heading towards the children's' playground and join a tarmac path
which emerges into Queenswood Road. Keep right to the main road,
Queenswood Drive.

Cross, and turn left and walk ahead for 80 metres to Woodbridge
Garth on the right, a cul de sac which ends in a path behind gardens.
Go right here, soon leading into Morris Wood, a remnant oakwood.
Keep in the same direction through the wood, but at a junction path,
take the path, half left, which leads to the stone footbridge over the
railway line in the opposite corner of the wood. This emerges in
Kepsthorn Close. Bear right then left at the junction to Spen Road.
Cross, and enter the recreation ground opposite. Walk across or
around the edge of the fields to the far right-hand corner where you'll
see Vesper Gate, a pillar of stone which is a surviving fragment of
the great gateway of Kirkstall Abbey. Keep ahead by the Vesper Gate
pub to cross Abbey Road (carefully) to where almost directly opposite a gap in the wall brings you into Kirkstall Abbey grounds. Turn
left along the footpath to the Abbey itself.

Kirkstall Abbey was founded 1152 by the Cistercians, as a daugh-
ter house of Fountains Abbey, and its main buildings, of an impres-

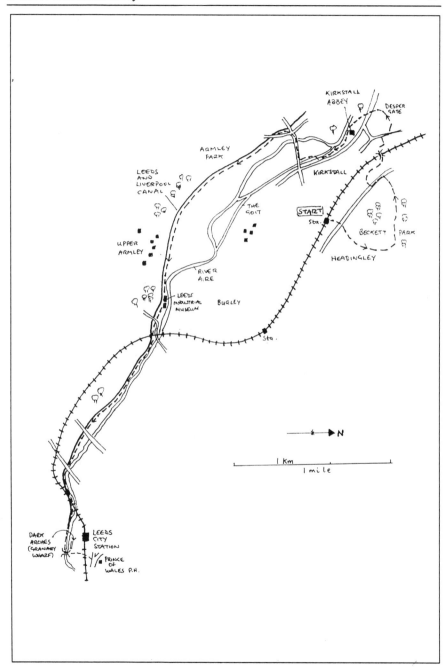

Kirkstall Abbey

sive scale, were completed between 1152 and 1182, stone being brought from the quarries at nearby Bramley Fall. The ruins, including much of the massive stone tower are remarkably complete, and represent the finest early Cistercian ruin in Britain.

It's worth spending a few minutes to enjoy the ruins, set in pleasant riverside parkland, a setting much appreciated by Romantic artists in the past, including J.M.W. Turner. The Abbey House Museum on the opposite side of Kirkstall Road is situated in the former Abbey Gate-house. Much original masonry remains as well as additions during its long life as a farmhouse and family home. It was purchased by Leeds City Council in 1927 who opened it as a folk museum, now notable for its carefully recreated 1890s street of period shops.

To continue the walk, make your way to the riverside and follow the path around the outside of the abbey, past the weir, the present weir dating from the 18th century and almost certainly replacing a monastic one. The path bears left and continues through the Abbey grounds, following the Abbey Mills mill race or goit, crossing a footbridge and remains of the Abbey Mills, and going alongside the Kirkstall Light Railway, a miniature railway line which operates at weekends.

You emerge in Bridge Mills, by the Home Furnishing Centre. Directly opposite is a tall Georgian building with bow windows, now a club. This is the former Star and Garter inn, a former stage coach inn on the old Leeds-Bradford and Leeds-Kendal turnpikes. Famous guests to stay here last century included the great actress Sarah Siddons.

Turn right past the Bridge Inn to cross the river. Cross the road at the traffic lights and go left over the railway into Broad Lane and left again into Wyther Lane, crossing to where a gap on the right leads to a footpath to join the tow-path of the Leeds Liverpool Canal.

Turn left here, following the tow-path which skirts the 73 acre Gott's Park, a fine estate which was the home of wealthy Leeds woollen manufacturer Benjamin Gott, who lived in Armley House, a magnificent Greek revival mansion which still stands in an estate – now Armley Park – created by leading landscape architect Humphrey Repton in 1810.

You pass Redcote Bridge, the rear exit from the Gott's estate, and are soon walking past the site of the former Kirkstall Power Station, demolished in 1986, and now part of a proposed Kirkstall Valley Nature Area. The tow-path crosses over twin bridges over a canal inlet where barges loaded with South Yorkshire coal once served the power station – this is now a small marina. The canal now goes underneath the railway line and, once again close to the river with its massive weir, reaches Armley Mills.

This massive mill complex was originally a fulling mill built soon after the Dissolution of the Monasteries, and by the 18th century, corn as well as textile mills occupied the site to utilise the powerful river currents and fall of water at this point. Later in the century the works were further developed to create a major water-powered wool treatment complex. These in turn which were much expanded under the ownership of Benjamin Gott in 1805-7 to create, at that time, the largest mill of its kind in the world. It now houses the Leeds Industrial Museum, a magnificent four-storey Museum devoted to various aspects of Leeds industrial past, including textiles, tailoring, engineering, printing, (there is even a light railway) and the early cinema, with a huge working water-wheel. Steps from the canal tow-path lead into the drive to the main Museum entrance.

From the Museum, it's an easy level walk into the city centre. Full information about the many fascinating buildings and bridges of the past is to be found in the Leeds Waterfront Heritage Trail available at Armley or Kirkstall Museums. But key features include the elegant Leeds and Thirsk Railway Viaduct which now carries the Harrogate Line across the Kirkstall Valley, Giant's Hill (soon afterwards) on the right where there was once a Norman Castle, remnants of the old Leeds Forge also on the right, and tanneries on the left, the Spring Gardens Lock, Greenwood and Batley's Factory, Oddy's Lock with striking wall murals close by, as well as typical canalside cottages, and the handsome Castleton Mills. You finally curve into the city

Leeds waterfront

centre through an area which is surprisingly green in terms of grass and shrubs, including willows by the river. Go under Wellington Road Bridge, with a complex of former early railway buildings, including a round-house to the right, and Monk Bridge, then the disused Leeds-Thirsk Railway viaduct which once carried crack steam expresses between Leeds and London into the old Leeds Central Station. As you sweep into the city, river, canal and railway in parallel, and go under the railway lines into City Station, you'll notice the twin red-brick Italianate brick campanile towers belonging to the Tower Works on the right.

Keep ahead directly into Leeds Canal Basin, past the old Leeds-Liverpool Canal Office before bearing left into Granary Wharf, walking out along the dramatic subterranean river bridge underneath the Dark Arches. Turn left at the main exit into Neville Street and cross at the pedestrian lights into Bishopgate. Directly ahead, on the corner of Mill Hill, you'll see the Prince of Wales tavern.

Walk 8: Hawksworth Woods and Newlay

An ideal summer evening or winter afternoon walk, this five mile stroll includes some remarkable surviving stretches of ancient Pennine oakwoods, so very close to busy north Leeds suburbs around Horsforth and the Kirkstall Valley.

Distance: 8km (5 mls)

Maps: Landranger 104; Pathfinder 683

Start: Horsforth Station

Finish: Headingley Station

Getting there: Frequent MetroTrain services on the Harrogate Line. Motorists can park at Horsforth Station car park and return to their cars by train.

The Pub

The Abbey at Newlay Bridge (0113 258 1248) dates from the mid 18th century, when it served travellers crossing Newlay Bridge as well as local quarrymen, forgemen and dyers from the nearby dyeworks. In late times it was close to the site of the old Horsforth and Newlay Station whose commuters it also once served. A Whitbreads house, it is open all day, and has a pleasant ambience with cask Whitbread Trophy, Castle Eden and Boddington's usually on offer, plus the occasional guest beer. Food usually available.

The Walk

From Horsforth Station's Harrogate-bound platforms, cross the car park to Station Road, crossing almost immediately ahead into Troy

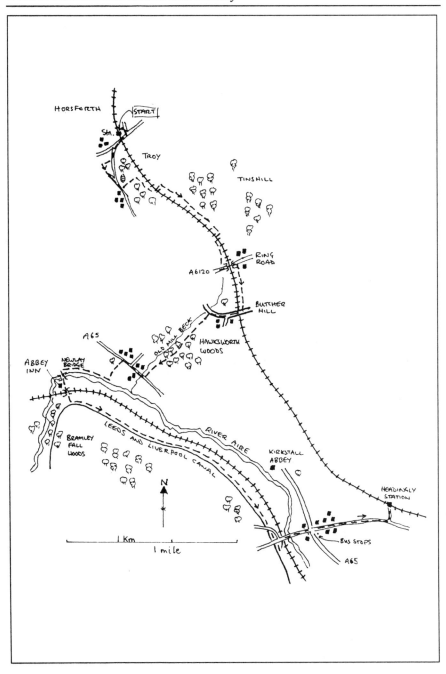

Road, but soon bear right opposite Mill House up a gravelly track on Troy Hill. Head towards a fine stone house. Look carefully and, alongside the railings on the left, a crude top step leads into a narrow enclosed path between hedge and railings, through an impressive tall kissing gate. Keep ahead to where this little right of way emerges on Lister Hill by offices. Go left downhill, the steps leading back into what is now Low Lane.

Cross the road carefully (traffic travels too fast) and turn right for 120 metres past a car showroom to the first opening on the left, with a tall footpath sign, which leads into Brookfoot, at the bottom of which by new offices, a metal barrier gives pedestrian access to a path into the woods, which crosses Old Mill Beck at a massive slab bridge. This is the first of a succession of surprisingly unspoiled ancient woods, mainly oak, passed on this walk, remnants of the kind of gritstone woodlands that covered the whole Pennine region in pre-industrial times. In this particular area are complex remains of old water-powered mills dating back probably to the 17th century, traces of which can still be discovered, including the old mill pond.

Keep straight ahead on the main path, bearing gently right along what becomes a cobbled way climbing up to the railway embankment, by a gap stile and old walls to reach a tunnel under the railway. Go through the tunnel but fork right into the woods rather than going ahead into the Tinshill housing estate.

Your path, narrow and a little muddy in places, keeps close to the railway embankment now for some 400 metres, passing but ignoring two more tunnels, before, at some fairly impenetrable scrub, it branches to the left and climbs gently uphill through a small clearing to meet a crossing path opposite Woodside Quarry, a large old sandstone quarry. Turn right here and descend down a narrow path over a stone arch bridge over the railway, and turn sharp left, again close to and alongside the stone wall and railway, following the path through oak woods and emerging at the busy Ring Road alongside the railway bridge.

Cross this road – where traffic goes at motorway speeds – with extreme care, turning left under the railway bridge, but sharp right immediately beyond the bridge where the path continues between houses and the railway into yet another wood, soon emerging at Butcher Hill behind Abbey Grange school.

Turn right down Butcher Hill, back over the railway, crossing with the pavement and past the junction to where on the left, near the bottom of the hill, a path leads into Hawksworth Wood, a shallow valley with Old Mill Beck below on the right. There was once an glass works in this wood. Keep straight ahead through another lovely stretch of woods for some 600 metres before eventually emerging on Abbey Road (A65) where just to the right, you'll see a refuge in the centre of the road to make crossing easier.

Turn right for some 250 metres to where just past a mock-Tudor lodge, a track on the left, Rein Road, signed as a bridle-path, descends to the side of the River Aire. Follow it as it curves right, again through lovely overhanging woods, to emerge by a cluster of cottages, at The Outwood.

Turn left at the junction over the now pedestrianised Newlay Bridge. Dating from 1819 this former toll bridge is one of the oldest iron bridges in the country. A bridge has existed across the River Aire at this point probably since monastic times, replacing the ancient dangerous "Horse-forth" or ford across the river. The present bridge was built at Shelf Iron works and was paid for by John Pollard, a local landowner. Walk ahead across the bridge, then over the much more modern bridge over the newly electrified Airedale railway line to where on the right, steps lead down to the Abbey Inn.

From the pub, return to the lane and bear right towards the canal, but take the waymarked path left which leads into a small and attractive picnic area. Continue along the path as it joins the towpath of the Leeds-Liverpool Canal by Newlay Locks.

Easy, fast walking down along the canal past lovely Bramley Fall Woods on the left, whose top quality gritstone was once extensively quarried and taken by river or canal for use for major building projects throughout Britain, including Kirkstall Abbey itself. The huge complex of factories and workshops on the left, is Kirkstall Forge, established in the 16th century in post-monastic times and still manufacturing, amongst other things, heavy axles for the motor industry; perhaps one of the oldest engineering works in England still in use, though the modern plant bears little resemblance to the 18th century water-powered forge whose trip hammers still survive within the modern factory complex.

Keep ahead past Forge Locks and the fertile fields of the flood plain which was used for many years for growing that West Riding speciality and delicacy, rhubarb, once exported from the area by the trainload. You soon pass Kirkstall Abbey and its estate largely concealed by the railway on your left. Continue ahead as you reach the first road bridge carrying the old Leeds-Bradford turnpike, reaching the massive, recently restored buildings of the old Kirkstall Brewery whose fine ales were once exported by canal and steamship via Goole to Australia and New Zealand. Immediately past the second road bridge, where Broad Lane crosses, take the path left which leads into Wyther Lane by the junction. Cross and keep right over Kirkstall Bridge to Kirkstall traffic lights. Cross at the lights to where (on the right) you can either catch a (frequent) bus into central Leeds or continue uphill along Kirkstall Lane for another 400 metres to Headingley Station for trains to Leeds or back to Horsforth.

Walk 9: Farsley and Rodley

A short but varied walk in west Leeds – with an amazing mixture of urban, suburban and surprisingly rural scenes, through urban ginnels, little known parks and a particularly delightful section of central Airedale.

Distance: 7km (4 mls)

Maps: Landranger 104; Pathfinder 683

Start: New Pudsey Station (Calderdale Line)

Finish: Horsforth New Road Side (frequent buses to Leeds).

Public Toilets: In Rodley.

Getting there: Frequent Metrotrain service between Leeds and Bradford Interchange calls at New Pudsey Station. This walk can also be extended down the canal tow-path to Kirkstall from Newlay Bridge (Walk 8 – 3km) or to the centre of Leeds (Walk 7 – 7km). Motorists should park in Leeds and take the train, returning to Leeds city centre by bus.

The Pub

The Rodley Barge, Rodley. Lovely old stone canalside pub on the Leeds Liverpool Canal, with its own waterfront, once serving ale and food to bargees, but now to boat owners and strollers who use the canal for leisure rather than cargo. Free House, with Stones, Worthington and well-kept Tetley Mild. Food most lunchtimes.

The Walk

From New Pudsey Station (Bradford bound platforms) take the exit leading to the Owlcotes Shopping Centre – a tarmac path alongside the railway for some 300 metres. But where this path bears right

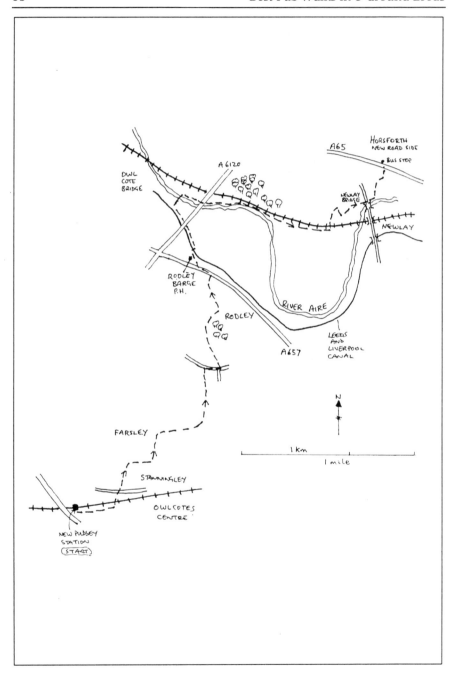

towards the shops, take the path left through a tunnel under the railway. Turn sharp right beyond the tunnel alongside the railway for 100 metres, before going left along a short street into the main Bradford Road.

Cross the road, turning right, but take the first turn left, New Street, past a large drive-in warehouse/store, at the end of which there is an entrance to a small park, West Royd Park. Enter by the gates, bearing right past shrubbery and lawns, passing a fine, if neglected, Victorian stone mansion, now an Arts Centre, before crossing to a path at the eastern edge of the park alongside a fence. Turn left along this tarmac path by tall garden fences. This becomes a ginnel which crosses Newlands between bungalows into the Boulevard by a recreation ground. Turn right alongside the recreation ground, passing cricket and soccer grounds, the path bearing right before it descends into a grassy hollow between housing estates, through which a public right of way runs. Turn left along here, through an area known as Farsley Beck Bottom, though the beck isn't really in view. The path makes its way along the Bottom, reaching a complex of mill buildings, following a ginnel alongside the buildings to emerge on Coal Hill Road. Turn right here, going uphill to Coal Hill Road's junction with Half Mile Lane. Take a path opposite this junction on the left which leads by a school playing field, following the edge of a hillside above gardens and narrow field enclosures. There are some fine open views ahead across the Aire Valley, as you curve round underneath pylons into an area of open scrubland. Several paths radiate from here – your path is to the left, following the slope before descending into Club Lane, a suburban street leading down into Town Street in Rodley.

Rodley is another of those outlying mill villages which still keep its identity though they are now part of a greater regional city complex. It was not only famous for its mills but also heavy engineering works, most notably boilermakers Pool Boiler Systems which still dominate Town Street, and the now vanished Booth and Smith Cranes, steam powered dock and railway cranes, exported world-wide, examples of which you'll still see in the Leeds Industrial Museum at Armley. Its cluster of Georgian and Victorian

The Rodley Barge

cottages, including three storey cottages along the canalside, help retain Rodley's distinctive character.

Turn left along Town Street for some 300 metres to the junction with Canal Road where, on the right, you'll find the Rodley Barge Inn.

From the pub follow Canal Road past the raised stone wharf which was once the site of a warehouse storing goods unloaded from barges, to the swing bridge and cross by the dock area past what is now a small marina packed with leisure craft. Turn left and follow the tow-path under Calverley Bridge which carries the Leeds Ring Road, continuing for another 200 metres to where, near Owl Bridge, steps on the right lead down from the tow-path into a cobbled lane, from where a flagged path branches left down to a fine old stone arched bridge over the River Aire. Once across the river turn sharp right down a stile and steps which lead to the riverside.

Now follows a beautiful stretch of riverside footpath, soon going under a massive concrete bridge carrying the A6120 Ring Road. The path gradually approaches the embankment of the Airedale railway line, soon squeezing between river and railway, before ascending and leaving the river at a copse, and climbing steeply to the left, over a stile, still alongside the railway, to where another stile gives access to a stone bridge across the electrified railway line which now runs through in a deep cutting.

Cross, turning right into Newlaithes Road, taking the first turn right into Newlay Grove, a pleasant suburban avenue. This descends and turns left, leading into Newlay Lane just north of Newlay Bridge. Turn right, but unless you choose to extend the walk along the canal tow-path down Airedale to Kirkstall, (see walk 8) don't cross the old bridge, instead follow the track, left, parallel to the river, The Rein. After 80 metres you reach a junction of tracks by houses – turn left uphill along a narrow path which is known as the Newlay Bridle-path. Follow it uphill until it emerges at Horsforth New Road Side. Cross at the pedestrian lights and turn right to the Metro bus stop for frequent buses to the centre of Leeds.

Walk 10: Cockersdale, Tong and Fulneck

This walk goes through some of the loveliest and least well-known countryside west of Leeds – from Farnley Park through Sykes Wood and Cockersdale, to explore ancient packhorseways to the still unspoiled villages of Tong and Fulneck.

Distance: 12km (8 mls)

Maps: Landranger 104; Pathfinder 683

Start and Finish: Old Farnley Bus terminus

Public Toilets: Farnley Park

Getting there: Bus service 42 from Eastgate or City Square (Wellington Street Stop) provides a half hourly service to Old Farnley, Sundays included. A choice of other services, including several cross-city bus routes (e.g. 43, 47, 66), also serve this terminus. Motorists should park in the public car park in Farnley Park – saving approximately half a mile – one kilometre – of the walk.

The Pub

The Greyhound in Tong (0113 285 2427) is a traditional long, low 17th century village pub, with mullioned windows and dripstones, and an unusual dovecot on the eastern end gable. A Tetley's house with Tetley Bitter and Mild on offer and at the time of our visit, Burton Bitter as a guest beer. The fire in the Victorian style room may be a clever imitation, but everything else is real – the grandfather clock, stone floor and remarkable collection of Toby jugs that decorate the long bar. A choice of bar meals is available in the small restaurant including Lasagne and a Venison Bake, but note that this is a pub which at time of writing closes at 3pm daily – reopening evenings.

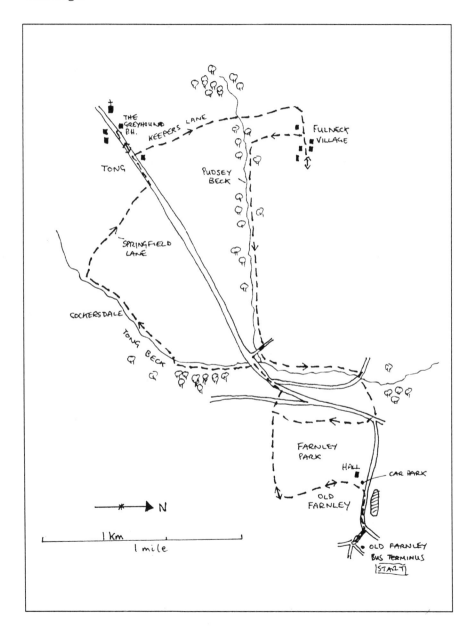

The Walk

From Old Farnley Bus terminus, head westwards through the remnants of this old village, not quite overwhelmed by housing estates, along Cross Lane, ignoring the junctions with Stonebridge Road and Butts Lane on the right and Chapel Lane on the left, until you reach the wide entrance to Farnley Park.

Enter the park (the car park where motorists will join the walk is on the right) noting the elegant Georgian mansion of Farnley Hall with its Tuscan Columns to the right. The mansion is now a museum store, but the park is graced by flower beds and rose gardens which are worth strolling through. The main route is the clear path which swings away to the left before the picnic tables through tall woods, past a toilet block, heading southwards through the mature beech woods which form the edge of the park to the sad graffiti covered entrance gates.

Turn sharp right here, along a narrow path which follows the stone estate wall. Keep along this path across stiles, ignoring the path that crosses from New Farnley on the left, the name given to the little mining village outpost of Farnley along the main Halifax road which is now covered by a new housing estate.

The path finally emerges at the corner wall of the estate where there is a fine viewpoint over the Cockersdale valley across to the town of Pudsey with its dominant church tower.

Turn sharp left to follow a grassy way along the edge of the ridge which goes below Park- side farm, bearing left before reaching a stile into a track with a tall waymark post. Turn left here down to Back Lane, a busy road. Turn right along the sidepath, crossing where it ends to continue at the other side to where a tall footpath sign indicates a fieldside path on the left. Go down a flight of steps and along the edge of the field, past a stables and over a stile to reach a stile into Tong Lane.

Cross carefully here (another fast road) to the sidepath, turning left downhill. Continue past the junction with Roker Lane, cross to the bridleway entrance and signs into Sykes wood on the left. Once through here, ignore the steps ahead but turn sharp right through the kissing gate (marked with a yellow waymark) which leads into a beautiful narrow path through the edge of Sykes Wood and into Cockersdale.

Follow the valley for about 400 metres to where a footbridge on the right crosses Cockersdale Beck. Cross, bearing left uphill to a wooden step stile which leads to a narrow way. Look carefully and you may notice that this is in fact the line of an old railway – other green narrow embankments also indicate their origin as former narrow gauge industrial lines serving what were originally iron works and later fireclay brickworks last century.

Cockersdale, once a hive of industrial activity, is now a remarkably renatured area of woodland. It is difficult to imagine that this unspoiled countryside is situated almost exactly between two of the North's largest cities, Leeds and Bradford.

Follow the path as it crosses stiles, all waymarked with yellow arrows and the little owl of the Leeds Country Way waymark, as it descends to the little beckside, keeping to the right bank, ignoring paths which spur off to the right and left over a footbridge. After about a mile in total (2km) from Tong Road, the path eventually reaches a T-junction with a track deep in the woods. Turn sharp right, uphill, with the blue bridle-path ignoring a kissing gate on the left. This soon becomes a deep sunken old packhorseway, Springfield Lane, with a paved way or "causey" for much of its length, ascending through arching trees and shrubs out of the Cockersdale valley, before soon passing a Gas company enclosure, then joining a metalled track which emerges at the eastern end of Tong Village.

Cross the road and turn left along the sidepath into the village, noting the little pinfold, and lion pump on the road near the corner of Keeper Lane.

Tong, which is just across the boundary in Bradford, has kept its rural character, with some delightful cottages and farm buildings as well as the Greyhound Inn, soon reached on the left hand side. But it's worth walking another 250 metres to see Tong Church, a delightful Georgian church. An ancient chapel on the site was entirely rebuilt in 1727 by Sir George Tempest of Tong Hall though some

Tong church

medieval features remain. Notable are the three decker pulpit, the 18th century pews, gallery and fittings, and outside the church, the stocks.

Return from church and pub back to Keeper Lane at the east side of the village. This lane (note Bradford's metric footpath signs) passes a fine Jacobean house at Hill Green. Where the tarmac swings left, the way is slightly left by stile and gate as Keeper Lane descends into the valley formed by Pudsey Beck. This is another lovely packhorse way, a fine recently restored causeway keeping walkers away from the track of horses (and an object lesson for countryside managers on how to do it) as the way descends steeply into the valley bottom to a footbridge. Follow the waymarks on the tall post up in the same direction up to Fulneck, the bridleway getting increasingly narrow between high banks as it ascends past the golf course. At a junction with two houses "Twenty Five and Twenty Six" keep slightly right uphill, on the stone flags. This emerges on a quiet lane. Turn right along the lane into the entrance of Fulneck Village. Walk into the village.

This curious village was established on land purchased by the Reverend Benjamin Ingram "a zealous preacher of the Gospel" in 1742. Soon afterwards it was settled by Moravian Bretheren, a small Protestant Sect established in Moravia, Central Europe (now part of the Czech Republic) who came to England in the 1720s. The settlers "soon began to erect three large buildings in one line; that in the middle being a chapel..., having a house for single men on one side and for single women on the other." Other houses followed include a house for widows, two family houses, a school and a "fine gravelled Walk".

The community thrived, and the schools, for Boys and for Girls, are now celebrated Independent Schools which are passed on the left. There is also the old shop which is now a shop, cafe and restaurant. Among the cottages on the left is a small Museum (open in the summer months). The little Moravian church with its bell tower can still be seen, still separating the two houses for men and women. Among celebrated inhabitants of the village was Pudsey-born cricketing legend Sir Len Hutton whose granny lived in a cottage in the village.

After you've had time to explore the village, the route continues along a footpath which starts at the western side of the school, where the entrance to the Golf Club descends between the main school buildings and a new red brick building, just below the circular stone wall of the car park. The path (not signed) descends along a narrow way, Dyehouse Lane, between trees to the left, again with a lovely old causeway, narrow and enclosed between high hedges alongside the golf course.

You emerge on the golf course. As a warning notice at the far side of the path suggests, do not cross the golf course if golfers are teeing off over the fairway. Look to your right and, when safe, cross straight to the banks of Pudsey Beck ahead, the public path – the Leeds Country Way, follows the banks of the Beck. Turn left. It isn't as pretty here as in Cockersdale, but still a pleasant path, crossing below the remains of a derelict mill at South Park, through open pastures usually occupied by horses and finally reaching Roker Lane after over a kilometre, at another complex of mill buildings.

Cross Roker Lane and turn right to go 100 metres to where a path (signed) by the bridge, goes down steps to the riverside. Another attractive, narrow beckside path now leads over more stiles, past old mills and weirs, to Troydale. Ignore the concrete stile on the left at Troydale Recreation Centre car park, but keep right through a wooden kissing gate to a picnic area and playground and along the stone embankment into Troydale Lane just below Troydale Mills. Cross and turn right once more, crossing the bridge and curving with the main road uphill. Now ignore the first signed path on the left into the wood, but take the second some 20 metres further up the lane, on some high stone flags. This path ascends wooden sleeper steps to a crossing path – turn left here through the oakwoods, but bear right at the fork. At the next junction, take the path sharp right up more wooden sleeper steps to a stile and narrow enclosed way which ascends to the junction with Tong Road and Hall Lane at the Beaulah Inn – another popular Tetley's pub with another chance of a pint if you missed out at Tong.

But the path continues almost exactly opposite the Beaulah on Hall Lane, at a wooden stile and is waymarked. Climb the field, bearing half right, towards the 1930s house above, ignoring the opening into the field on the right, but climbing above and around the bramble hedge in the same the field, keeping right, and descending slightly to a narrow, not very obvious post stile leading into scrubby woodland on the right. The path climbs into woodland, passing a ruined cattle-shed and ascending to a stile in a narrow lane.

Turn right here, and continue to where the tarmac bears right where your path, waymarked, keeps straight ahead through a gap stile in the fence. About 100 metres further on, where the path bears slightly right above an enclosure with keep out notices, notice a stone post on the left which looks like an old gatepost but is in fact an old packhorseway guidestoop. Though much weathered and faded, the keen amateur archaeologist might just be able to decipher the remains of 17th century lettering, Halifax on one side and Ilkley and Wakefield – in opposite directions – on the other. This is a reminder that this forgotten little path once formed a junction on a once busy packhorse ways between these three ancient Yorkshire towns.

Continue along the lane by blackthorn which soon reaches the wall enclosing Farnley Park. Keep ahead to the estate wall corner passed in the earlier part of the walk, this time turning left along the outside of the Estate Wall and back into the Park for the car park and Old Farnley bus terminus for frequent buses back into the city centre and beyond.

Walk 11: Churwell and Morley

Unusual panoramic views across the whole of the city of Leeds are the exceptional features of this easy walk in the south west of the city, mainly along farm tracks, through elevated areas of attractive Green Belt between West Leeds and the old township of Morley.

Distance: 7km (4 mls)

Maps: Landranger 104; Pathfinders 683, 692

Start: Old Farnley Bus terminus

Finish: Morley Station (Huddersfield Line) or Town Hall bus terminus

Getting there: Frequent bus services from Eastgate or Wellington Street (42, 43); hourly return trains from Morley or choice of bus service from Morley Town Hall. Motorists should park in Leeds and use the bus.

The Pub

The New Inn, Churwell (0113 253 3468). Friendly Victorian pub on Elland Road with stone flagged floor and comfortable lounge – CAMRA listed. Known as the "Bottom 'Ole" to distinguish it from other pubs in Churwell. Boddington's, Whitbread Trophy, Moorhouses' Pendle Witch and guest beer are usually available – food most times of day. Open all day.

The Walk

From Old Farnley Bus head westwards along Cross Lane, ignoring the junctions with Stonebridge Road and Butts Lane on the right and Chapel Lane on the left, until the wide entrance into Farnley Park.

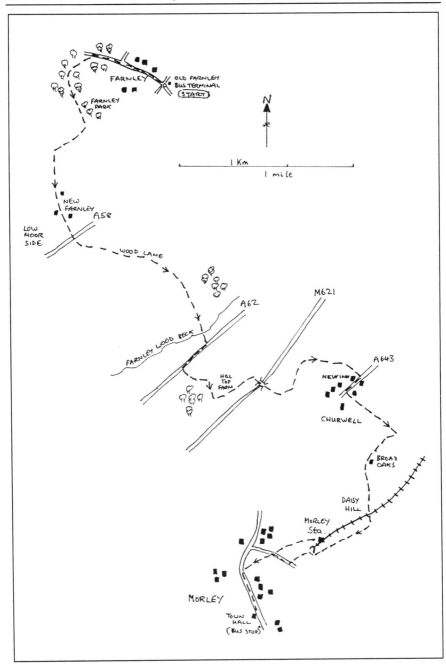

Enter the park. Follow the drive to the car park area, bearing left before the picnic tables to join a path which heads southwards through the mature beech woods which form the edge of the park to the southern entrance gates.

Turn sharp right here, along a narrow path which follows the stone estate wall. Keep along this path and through a stile, about 50 metres beyond this, take the path on the left which crosses the fields to twin stiles ahead (ignore the third stile on the right) becoming a paved causeway across long forgotten mine tailings, leading into Castle Ings Gardens at New Farnley. Ignore paths to the right, but follow Castle Ings Green as it bears left by new bungalows. At its junction with Ennerdale Way two concrete finger posts mark the start of a footpath on the right which follows a grassy route which edges past the backs of gardens. This emerges on the busy A58 at Low Moor Side.

Cross carefully. Directly ahead by the 30mph sign is the entrance to Wenworth Farm. Take this tarmac track as it immediately bends left, following a low ridge with increasingly impressive views across the lower Aire Valley- you'll soon be looking across the whole of Leeds in its gigantic bowl between the hills, with the University Clock Tower, City Hall and the Town Hall (in front of tall office blocks) as prominent landmarks – the latter rarely seen in views across Leeds. Behind to your left you'll see the Pudsey Church and to the right, also on a hilltop, the proud tower of Morley Town Hall, your ultimate destination, this being one of the few points where all three landmarks are visible.

Follow the track past Wood End farm to a fork. Take the right fork, the narrower way which runs between fences. This is a lovely old bridleway which swings southwestwards with ever more open views across the skyscraper blocks of South Leeds to Middleton Woods in the distance down to Farnley Wood Beck, and a little wooded hollow to emerge at the main A62 by scruffy industrial buildings. Turn right past the curious factory warehouse/scrapyard known as St. Bernard, crossing the A62 carefully to a concrete track on the left with a No Through Road sign. Take this past restored tips and over an old railway bridge, crossing the line of a long vanished trackbed, heading towards the white cottages ahead where, at a cross roads, you turn right past the cottages and ascend to another cross roads. The way is now sharp left over a stile by a metal gate which climbs past the derelict Hill Top Farm. Keep ahead as the track crosses the brow of the hill before descending by the M621 motorway and another crossing of paths. Turn right to go through the motorway tunnel, continuing at the other side along and around the edge of a field to where, on the left, a narrow path leads over a little wooden plank bridge over a dyke to the edge of a new housing estate. Follow a new gravel path left uphill, behind the estate, but at the next junction turn left again along a new stretch of path which curves behind the housing. At a fork in the path, however, take an older, grassy path branching left to a gap stile. This leads to a path well-eroded by scrambling bikes, up another long abandoned spoil tip which forms a low cliff above the shallow valley carrying the motorway.

On the right is a wire fence forming a long enclosure. Follow the fence round, eventually curving right between the fence and allotments. At an estate road, cross by the metal safety barrier, continuing along a narrow, attractive ginnel which winds between gardens, snaking left then right before eventually emerging at a junction. Almost directly ahead is School Street. Pass Churwell Working Men's Club onto Elland Road. Turn right to the New Inn.

From New Inn cross Elland Road and turn right, but then take the road Little Lane, left just before The Golden Fleece, going first right into Back Green past Churwell Methodist Chapel then by a second old chapel, now a workshop. Beyond this old chapel is a footpath, narrow and enclosed between stone walls, which descends between fields, soon zigzagging to a field boundary crossing. Bear right up to the large barn and farm ahead – Broad Oak. Keep to the right-hand side of the farm to locate the farm track past farm buildings. Follow this track for 200 metres. Where it turns sharp right, take the fainter track sharp left, which descends to a hollow through which the Leeds-Huddersfield railway runs. Cross at the stile and cross over the tracks at the little level crossing with care – trains pass at high speed. Bear right along the track which now goes around the outside of industrial plant, Harder Bros and Orcol Fuels, past the southern side of Morley Station (no access from this side). As the lane hairpins round towards the station entrance, note the steps at the apex of the hairpin. Unless you are catching a train, take the steps uphill, turning right at the top past the Miners' Arms – a pleasant Tetley's pub – and along the road for some 350 metres to where, on the left, Troy Road slopes up to the centre of Morley.

Morley may now be part of Leeds but it has kept its essential character as a typical West Riding wool town, occupying an unusual hilltop site on a ridge above motorway and railway. There are some impressive millstone grit Victorian public and private buildings, churches, chapels, offices and houses, none more impressive than the Town Hall itself with its massive columns and huge tower capped by a classical dome. It was built in 1895 to the design of G.A. Fox. There's a market and shopping centre, more pubs, and lots of buses back to Leeds centre – and elsewhere. But if you prefer to take the train for a fast, 12 minute ride to City Station, retrace your steps down Troy Road, turning left at the bottom, crossing and going first right down what appears to be a cul-de-sac track, but which ends in steps leading into Valley Road. Directly ahead is Morley Metrotrain station.

Walk 12: Yeadon Tarn, Rawdon Billing and Spring Woods

It's difficult to imagine that the City of Leeds exists in the lower part of a once richly wooded Yorkshire Dale; this circular walk in central Airedale gives a glimpse of just how beautiful Leeds' own dale still is – despite centuries of settlement and industrialisation.

Distance: 15km (9 mls)

Maps: Landranger 104; Pathfinders 671, 672, 682, 683; The Aireborough Footpath Map (Stile Maps)

Start & Finish (circular walk)**:** Guiseley Station (Wharfedale Line)

Getting there: Metrotrain to Guiseley. Motorists should park in Guiseley.

The Pub

The Emmot Arms, Rawdon (0113 250 6036). A traditional stone built Yorkshire pub, with low beams, an open fire in winter, friendly tap room and good beer – Sam Smith's, Old Brewery Bitter. Food available at the bar or in the restaurant – lunchtimes only. CAMRA listed.

The Walk

From Guiseley Station, if arriving from Leeds, cross the footbridge over the tracks to the Leeds-bound platforms and exit through the short alleyway between bungalows which forms the way out. Turn right into Netherfield Road for 50 metres to where a narrow enclosed ginnel (signposted) on the left leads between gardens and across an

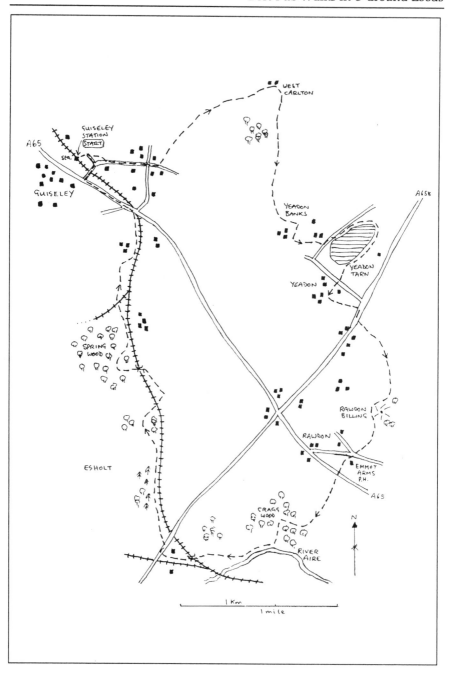

estate road. Follow it around until it reaches the main road, Oxford Road.

Turn left here, and walk along the busy road for some 400 metres past houses, shops and mills, past the junction with Town Street, to where, on the left a short section of track leads to a stile and a junction of paths. Turn left then first right over a stile to take a path which essentially follows a stream over stiles, along a series of small field enclosures. Following the stream to the right, over and through stiles, ascending slightly but, after around 500 metres, the path turns sharply right over a stile and a little footbridge, keeping the fence to the right. The path then turns left around the field corner for 80 metres before going through a stile on the right, and continues up the field for 120 metres, then right again through a gate heading to the wood ahead. Here the path now turns left then first right around the top of the wood to head across to West Carlton Farm.

At the farm, take the green, enclosed way which heads due south, over stiles, descending a hillside around the outside of the enclosures, then descending to the stream, before climbing towards the housing estate at Shaw Lane ahead. Continue climbing steeply up Yeadon Banks, again crossing a series of stiles between narrow enclosures. As you reach the housing estate, with a mill ahead, look for the narrow but well-used permissive path which climbs to the rim of the hilltop of the left – follow this, which leads over waste ground over the brow of the hill, with fine views, before descending to join Haw Lane.

Turn right here for around 100 metres, ignoring the junction with Leslie Avenue, but taking the next estate road, Hawthorn Drive, on the left. Follow this as it leads into Cemetery Road. Directly ahead you will see Yeadon Tarn and an entrance into the path around the Tarn. Turn left here to follow the path around the lake.

Yeadon Tarn is a little jewel – in effect a large mill pond which has become a popular sailing area, usually packed with the colourful sails of small yachts and dinghies, its perimeter path an even more popular Sunday stroll. Follow the path around the Tarn, leaving it at almost its most southerly point where a tarmac path leads into Dam Lane. Keep ahead into Yeadon High Street.

Yeadon Tarn

Cross, and walk along Windmill Lane, following it for some 250 metres to its junction with Grange Avenue. Turn left here, keeping ahead along a narrow ginnel which emerges on the A658 Harrogate Road. Cross with care and turn right for 100 metres. Then left next along Moorfield Drive, at the end of which a path bears left across a couple of small enclosures, then turns southwards down, then up two long fields, heading for the tree-crowned summit of Rawdon Billing ahead.

Follow the path up to the Billing – at the top stile bear right heading up to the summit enclosure, a little gritstone hill, partly quarried, which makes an exceptionally good viewpoint, a pano-rama across and along the Aire valley, taking in the whole of Airebrough, central Airedale, Horsforth, and even central parts of Leeds.

Follow the circular path round the Billing around to the south, going over the stile and down the narrow enclosed way southwards which descends into Rawdon. The track emerges into a lane, Billing

View, which meets Town Street, on the corner of which stands the Emmot Arms.

From the pub, follow the narrow lane almost opposite, Well Lane, which leads to the busy Leeds Road, A65 at Low Green Cross and directly ahead go down a narrow track, Cliff Lane, which leads past cottages to an attractive enclosed bridle-path. Follow the path down as far as you can go, straight ahead at the first junction into woodland to a T-junction of tracks. Turn right here along Woodland Drive, past the entrances to several grand houses, but left again at the next junction, by garden entrances, eventually descending the narrow way to the banks of the River Aire.

Right here, along the river for some 300 metres, but where the railway bridge comes into view, take a stile right which leads across a playing field to the exit behind the changing room. This leads by gate and stile into Woodlands Drive.

Keep ahead at the next junction, over the railway bridge carrying the Leeds branch of the Wharfedale line to the main Bradford-Harrogate Road. Cross, and walk uphill for some 100 metres to the entrance of Walk Hill Farm where a bridle-path heads due north along the edge of woodland, finding its way in a narrow strip of oakwoods – between the railway and Esholt sewage works, which, contrary to expectations, is a very attractive stretch of path, both railway and trees hidden by semi-natural Pennine oakwoods. Its name Nun Woods recalls the Nunnery which once existed at Esholt.

Follow this track for a kilometre – just over half a mile – to a junction of tracks. Turn right here along another pleasant wooded track leading under the railway, but turn sharp left at the next junction, the track now climbing alongside the newly electrified line. Left at the next junction over the railway bridge, then first right, the track now climbing as the railway climbs, above the little gorge formed by Guiseley Beck, soon going underneath yet another railway line – this time the Bradford branch of the scenic Wharfedale Line. Continue towards a housing estate and another T-junction. Turn right here walking back to the railway line from where a narrow ginnel leads alongside the railway fence into a housing estate. Keep ahead, in the same direction to where another ginnel goes alongside the line to join the main Leeds Road (A65) at Greenbottom in Guiseley.

Central Guiseley is now totally transformed by huge drive-in burger malls and supermarkets – no place for mere mortals on foot. Cross at the traffic lights to avoid the worst, and head back along the pavement to the Oxford Road traffic lights and Station ahead; the Station Inn beyond the lights (with one or two guest ales usually available) being a useful watering hole if there's a wait for a train.

Walk 13: Adel and Eccup

A walk in the Green Belt north of Leeds through countryside of remarkable beauty, taking in one of Britain's finest small Norman churches and an unspoiled hamlet on the edge of the Yorkshire Dales.

Distance: 8km (5 mls)

Maps: Landranger 104; Pathfinder 672

Start: Lawnswood Arms (Otley Road)

Finish: Bramhope village

Getting there: Buses 1, 1a from Briggate or 780, X87/784 from Leeds Bus Station. Alight at Holt Lane just before the Lawnswood Arms (A660). Return 780, X84/784 from Bramhope to Lawnwood Arms. Motorists should park in Holt Lane and return by bus to Lawnswood Arms.

The Pub

The New Inn, Eccup (0113 288 6335). A former farmhouse-style village beerhouse, this popular Tetley's pub has inevitably expanded to cater for a suburban lunchtime clientele, (with a welcome Family Room and outside beer garden and play area) but keeps its cosy public bar with the nearest to be seen in Leeds to a German-style "Stammtisch" – a table reserved for locals. "If you look like this," says a label over the bar corner settle, under a picture of an old farmer in time-worn jacket, "you may sit here". Gortex wearers need not be offended with Marston's Pedigree, Tetley Bitter and, when we called, excellent Tetley Mild on offer. Coffee always available, imaginative food (including vegetarian) at most times.

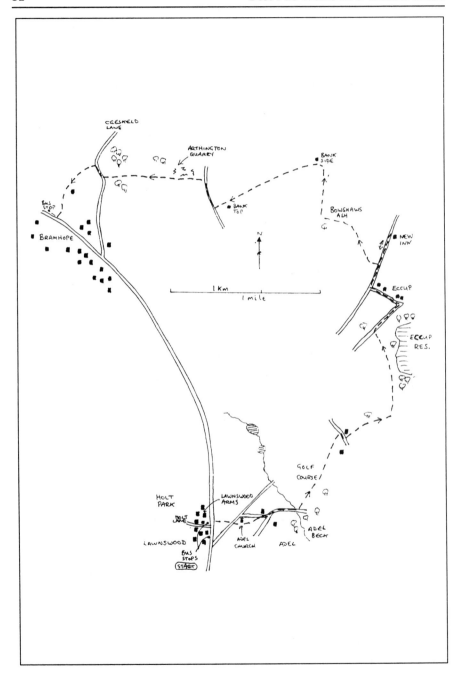

The Walk

From the Lawnswood Arms walk along Otley Road towards Otley for around 100 metres to where a large pillar of stone, dabbed with white paint, indicates where, directly opposite, there is a half hidden path (signed). Cross the frenzied, speeding traffic along the A660 with great care, to locate a stone step between the hedge leading into a field path. This is an ancient parishioners' way, probably as old as Adel Church itself, which goes back to Norman times. Cross the field, perhaps through arable crops but hopefully beaten down, to another stile and tiny bridge over a sike. The path now follows a headland past trees to emerge at Adel Church. Cross into the churchyard to go directly on the flagged path.

This beautiful little church was described by Nikolaus Pevsner as "one of the best and most complete Norman churches in Yorkshire", but in fact there are few finer examples of a small Norman church in Britain. Probably dating from the middle 12th century, one of its outstanding features is a richly carved doorway arch, full of carved

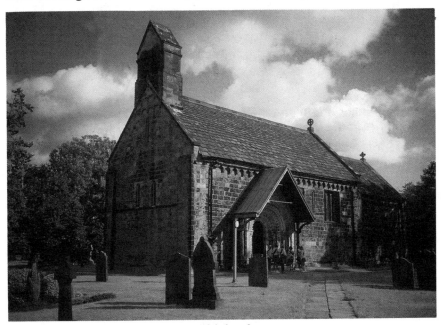

Adel church

figures of beasts and figurines which show the strong influence of a local Anglo-Saxon sculptural tradition.

Continue past the church on the flagged path to the eastern exit, keeping straight ahead on a narrow path between trees and shrubs which angles into Back Church Lane. Keep ahead to the junction with Long Causeway and Staircase Lane, going left downhill, but for once keeping to the left on the outside of the bend to avoid rat-running cars which speed through.

Once past the bridge in the beck bottom, an informal path on the left takes the walker off the tarmac but parallel with the road, going uphill to where just past the car park, serving Adel Woods, you join a wider track. Keep left along this path, which forms part of the Dales Way Link between Leeds and Ilkley.

Follow this path to where at a bridlegate and stile, it turns right. Then follow it along a hedge soon entering and skirting Headingley Golf Course, the walker protected by hawthorn hedges at either side. At King Lane, another surprisingly busy minor road, cross carefully to continue along the track to the right of the white farmhouse, now a golf club house. The path again skirts the edge of the golf course, through stiles, alongside a hedge, before descending to another stile and keeping ahead into fine open countryside, with a fence to the left.

At the second stile, a wooden stile on the fence on the left in the corner of the field, on the edge of a large field which leads to the plantations surrounding Eccup Reservoir, turn sharp left along a path parallel to the hedge which leads to a tongue of woodland. This meets and passes the permissive path around Eccup Reservoir (for a 5km – 2 mile extension to this walk, turn right here to follow the reservoir path around the reservoir, rejoining this walk at the path which leads up to Eccup village). The main route crosses stiles past the edge of the wood and then crosses a field to the lane, Eccup Moor Road.

Turn right here, descending to where the lane crosses a bridge over a little beck, immediately to the left of which a track leads uphill to the little hamlet of Eccup – still a remarkably preserved rural settlement, thanks both to good Green Belt policies and the restrictive limits on development (for anti-pollution reasons) by the old Leeds Corporation Water Board – though unmistakeable signs of suburbanisation are creeping in.

Turn right in the lane, Eccup Lane, walking on the right to face oncoming traffic, soon passing Brookland Farm, 50 metres beyond which a stile and signposted path beckons – this is the continuation of the route – after calling at the New Inn which is another 350 metres ahead.

From the pub, suitably refreshed, return back to the stile north of Brookland Farm, crossing to the next stile in the field corner ahead, but instead of going straight ahead on what looks like the obvious path (and is better waymarked), turn sharp right over a wooden step stile where you will see a far less obvious waymark. This path, still the Dales Way link path, follows the field edge, by the fence on the right, then crosses the field end to another stile, bearing left, this time with the hedge to the left. Continue for 400 metres, having crossed another stile to a second stile where the path, not waymarked, goes sharp right past Bowshows Ash.

This path follows the brow of the hill, and suddenly a magnificent panorama of Wharfedale opens out below you – prominent landmarks being Almscliffe Crag on the skyline, Arthington Church and railway viaduct, with the Washburn Valley, Otley Chevin and Burley Moor to the west.

Descend the hill, still alongside the hedge to the stile below, crossing to the next stile, then following a narrow path across scrubland by Bank Side farm to where a tall wooden finger post indicates the Ebor Way and paths to both Eccup and Arthington. Turn left, now along the Ebor Way, to the stile and gate by the barn, soon entering a narrow, enclosed green way by a gate and stile, climbing uphill before eventually reaching and joining the farmtrack at Bank Top. Go straight ahead through the farm and past the farmhouse to Arthington Road.

Ignore the path straight ahead which carries the Dales Way to metalled roads into Bramhope, and turn right for 200 metres to where at the brow of the hill, a bridle-path leads along the southern perimeter of Arthington Quarry, a vast sandstone crater. In spite of this, this is a beautiful path, partially overgrown with young rowan trees, leading alongside and soon beyond the quarry, before curving left into a green bowl of the hills on the well-wooded edge of the Bramhope escarpment; the spire of Bramhope Church and the less aesthetic concrete bulk of the Leeds-Bradford Forte-Crest Hotel – a building as ugly as its name – notable landmarks ahead.

The bridle-path eventually joins the Creskeld Lane from Bramhope. Turn right again for another 200 metres to where on the left a bridleway sign indicates a lovely path which contours the hillside above and close to Bramhope Tunnel. This path ascends soon emerging as a drive leading into an estate road in Bramhope. Now keep straight ahead up what looks like a tarmac garden path, but is in fact the continuation of the ancient bridleway now almost – but not quite – obliterated by car-dominated suburbia. This ascends steeply between the wooden fences of gardens. At the next estate road the footpath has been diverted – turn left for 100 metres to where, at the bend of the road, a footpath sign indicates a path, right, which climbs up and around the back of the new houses, eventually joining the original line of footpath in scrubby woodland before ascending stone steps to the main A660 road.

A few metres to the right is the Metro stop with X84/784 buses back to Lawnswood Arms and Leeds. Check your times, as buses are every half hour on weekdays, hourly on Sundays. If you are between buses and, having checked your times, want to spend time in more comfortable surroundings, take the steps behind the northbound Metro bus stop leading into Bramhope Main Street. Turn right once there for 300 metres to The Fox and Hounds (see walk 15).

Walk 14: The Chevin

Leeds' only Forest Park occupies most of The Chevin, a long, gritstone ridge overlooking the old town of Otley, from the summit of which is a spectacular "Surprise View" along the length of Wharfedale which this walk takes full advantage of.

Distance: 10km – 6 mls

Maps: Landranger 104; Pathfinder 671

Start: Guiseley Railway Station

Finish: Otley

Public Toilets: The White House, Otley Chevin

Getting there: MetroTrain Wharfedale line from Leeds and Bradford to Guiseley; return X84/ 784 bus services back to Leeds. Motorists should park in Guiseley and catch bus 735 back to Guiseley.

The Pub

The Royalty on Yorkgate, Otley Chevin (01943 461156) developed last century from a former farmhouse that became a beerhouse and finally a small and friendly pub, with a Family Room, popular with walkers and locals alike. The name Royalty is nothing to do with Kings or Queens, but indicates a parcel or Royalty of land on which the farmhouse once stood. Tetley Bitter and Mild, and usually a guest beer such as Marston's Pedigree on offer, as well as a choice of food from snacks to full lunches in the adjacent dining areas.

The Walk

From Guiseley Station, if arriving from Leeds, cross the footbridge over the tracks to the Leeds-bound platforms and exit through the short alleyway between bungalows which forms the way out. Turn left into Netherfield Road for 400 metres, walking past impressive mill buildings to where, on the right a narrow footpath, signed, goes in front of a row of stone cottages – Greenshaw Terrace. Follow the enclosed way for 200 metres beyond the cottages, but as it bends right, go through the opening on the left to a path which leads into a grassy hillside towards a mill. This path forks before a bench – take the right fork uphill, ascending to a stile in the wall corner.

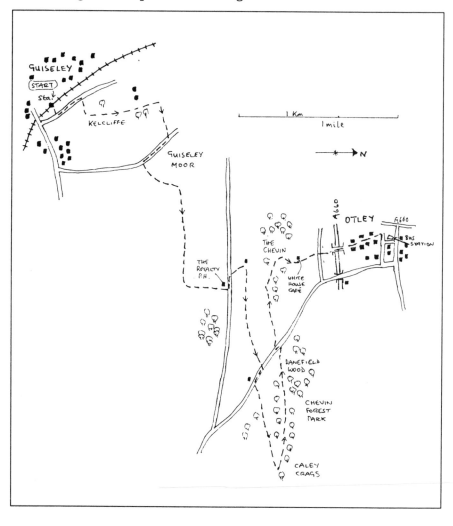

This enters a narrow track. Turn left, but almost immediately look for a stile on the right which continues the path in the same direction, diagonally across the next field, curving up and around a narrow embankment above suburban gardens at Kelcliffe, before heading to a gate and stile which leads to Bracken End Farm. There are fine views across the saddle which divides Airedale and Wharfedale, looking across to Burley Moor, dominated by the residential areas – as well as residual mills, reminder of Aireborough's textile heritage – but also with a magnificent rim of open moorland as a backcloth.

Follow the farm track to a T-junction of tracks. Turn right, uphill along a sandy way, ascending a steep, gorsey hillside, the track widening. This is the last unenclosed remnant of what was Guiseley Moor. You reach Moor Top Lane. Turn right here, walking along the lane for 400 metres past a disused quarry to a junction with a track where the lane bends. Turn left here, following the track up and past Moor Farm, turning northwards to where, after another 200 metres, there is another junction of tracks. Turn right and follow another long walled track past long, narrow enclosure fields, with distant views across farmland to the south across Aireborough and with the runway lights of Leeds-Bradford Airport coming into view. Continue, and after 900 metres – about half a mile – the track ends at a gate and narrow stile into a meadow. Cross, negotiating a swampy area by the gate – keeping close to the wall.

You will now see The Royalty, the white building on the crest of the hill to your left. In the left-hand corner of the enclosed field (used as a shooting range) white paint marks the path and stile. Cross directly to the stile, and follow close to the wall (especially if shooting is taking place which happens some weekends), to emerge in the beer garden.

From The Royalty, turn left along Yorkgate Road for 100 metres to enter the Beacon Gate Car park. Cross the car park to the stile in the wall which leads onto The Chevin itself – a point known for self evident reasons as Surprise View. The crags on the left mark the site of the Chevin Beacon, once part of the chain of beacons which crossed Britain and warned people against imminent invasion.

Remains of the Beacon Keeper's cottage can still be seen – this was known as Jenny's Cottage after one Jenny Veal who served teas there for walkers. A view-finder explains what can be seen looking across a magnificent panorama of Wharfedale and Otley below you, Almscliffe Crag prominent on the skyline to the west. The name Chevin is probably a Celtic name derived from "Cefn" meaning ridge. The Chevin is now the Leeds Forest Park, a semi wild area of glorious heathland, crag and woodland.

Paths lead directly downhill to Otley if you wish to shorten the walk – but that would be to miss perhaps the best sections of the walk. To enjoy them turn right, following the track along the ridge top to where it goes through Miller Lane Gate, a gate leading into the enclosed way Miller Lane, which descends to the main East Chevin road by Danefield House. Cross the road, but note the narrow stile opposite leading down to a narrow welcome permissive path through the woods which winds uphill parallel, but away from the road and its traffic, leading to York Gate car park. Tracks fork from here – take the left, lower of the two main paths eastward – the footpath not the Chippendale Ride bridleway straight ahead. This slopes towards beautiful woodland – and an attractive picnic area.

A frequent visitor to Wharfedale and The Chevin was J.M.W.Turner, (1775-1851) arguably England's greatest landscape painter, who made many watercolours of the area, and, it is now suggested, used Caley Crags and The Chevin as inspiration for his epic painting of Hannibal Crossing the Alps. This all forms part of the Danefield Estate, a fragment of the medieval Forest of Knaresborough which in 1946 was presented to the town of Otley and the City of Leeds by Major Horton-Fawkes of nearby Farnley Hall, and has been carefully maintained by the foresters and now the City Countryside service ever since.

Follow the path over Shawfield which dips steeply down steps to cross the Holbeck at a little footbridge, continuing by Stag Wood and keeper's Wood Plantation until it merges at a broader track at Caley Crag – another fine outcrop of millstone grit and another fine viewpoint.

Turn sharp left here, to descend the main track which descends through Poolscar Plantation and back across Holbeck, past foresters' cabins, gradually ascending to the Danefieldgate entrance back on East Chevin Road. Turn left uphill for 50 metres to the entrance to East Chevin Car Park, to the rear of which a pedestrian gate leads to another attractive section of path which climbs behind the old quarry to follow a narrow terrace, again with lovely forest views. Follow the track as it ascends then parallels the hillside, soon entering the woods and crossing the stone steps leading down into Otley, but keep directly ahead to the White House Visitor centre – a small Leeds Countryside Service Interpretative Centre with excellent tea rooms (open most days during the summer months and on winter Sunday afternoons) and toilets close by.

From the White House you can either retrace your route back to the steep steps which descend the hillside towards Otley, or take the easier driveway – both ways converge at the crossing of paths at White House Gate. Your path is the narrow, enclosed way leading slightly to the left which descends to a lane, Birdcage Walk, and continues over a long footbridge over Otley by-pass and the site of the town's much lamented Railway Station, an early and singularly ill-thought out victim of the Beeching Axe in 1965. Continue along Station Road with its typical railway period commuters' terraced houses.

The Bus Station is on the right, but most people will want to explore this very typical small Dales market town, with its cobbled market place, town clock donated by grateful World War I Belgian refugees, the fine medieval church, its memorial to cabinet-maker Thomas Chippendale (born in Otley in 1718) and for real ale seekers, an excellent choice of inns – the Junction and the Bay Horse are especially to be commended.

Walk 15: Along Bramhope Tunnel

This walk from the busy North Leeds suburban village of Horsforth to the ancient market town of Otley follows the line of a remarkable early Victorian railway tunnel which runs underneath the watershed that divides Airedale and Wharfedale.

Distance: 11km (7 mls)

Maps: Landranger sheet 104; Pathfinder sheets 683, 672

Start: Horsforth Railway Station

Finish: Otley Bus Station

Getting there: MetroTrain Harrogate line to Horsforth; return from Otley on bus services 780, 784 or X84. Motorists should park in Leeds and use the train and bus.

The Pub

The Fox and Hounds, Bramhope, (0113 284 2448) is a traditional village pub, dating from last century which, though it is now an extremely popular hostelry on the outskirts of a busy Leeds suburb, has kept its rural atmosphere. Excellent Tetley's bitter and mild on offer, as well as a guest beer, at time of our visit Marston's Pedigree. Food available most lunch times. Open all day Fridays and Saturdays, other days closing at 3pm until evening.

The Walk

From Horsforth Station cross the little car park accessible from the northbound platform, to join a track at the far side. Turn right past the high fence of a woodyard and DIY centre, along a track, keeping

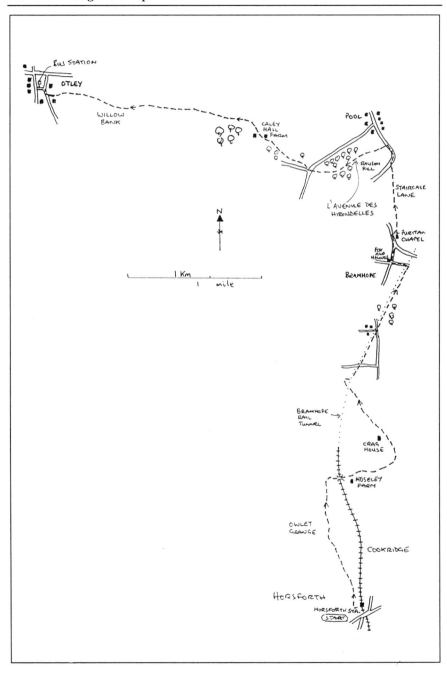

to the left of the woodyard office, behind house gardens. Where the track ends, a narrow path on the left leads into Sussex Avenue. Turn right off the lane end where a narrow stile leads into the field beyond.

Suddenly you are in open countryside, a landscape of little fields bounded by ancient drystone walls and old oak trees. The path, reasonably clear on the ground, bearing half left to another stile between short posts in the field corner, then slightly more sharply left to a similar stile, before bearing more to the right and heading to Ling Bob farm, where a stile by a gate takes the path alongside the wall by the farmyard (now a stables) with its collection of remarkable old farm buildings and barns.

Keep alongside the wall, over stiles to where the path joins the track from the farm, following the wall by the wood around the corner; 100 metres from the corner a path, on the right, leads over a narrow wooden stile and alongside a hedge and fence, the hedge on your left; a narrow causeway and stepping stones making progress a little easier. The path keeps in the same direction, alongside the hedge, towards Owlet Farm ahead where it dips down into the valley formed by Scotland Beck. It has been diverted here – follow the yellow waymarks to the right around the outside of a paddock, over the beck at a little footbridge and up the other side to rejoin the line of path, again, marked stiles, which now follow a tall hawthorn hedge before bearing right to join a deep sunken track below Dean Grange Farm. Turn right at this track, passing Nether Spring Cottage, down to the shallow valley, Moseley Bottom, the former by Moseley Beck. As you cross the railway, note the massive entrance to Bramhope Tunnel on the left.

Bramhope Tunnel was opened in 1849, and was formerly part of the Leeds-Thirsk Railway; a railway developed by Leeds merchants as a direct route to the north east to break the monopoly being established by George Hudson and his York and North Midland Railway. Bramhope Tunnel, 2 miles and 241 yards long, is still the eighth longest tunnel in Great Britain and with 23 men dying in its construction – a memorial to their sacrifice in the form of a stone model of the tunnel, is still to be seen in Otley churchyard. The line now only operates as far as Harrogate, but remains an important commuter railway with a single Inter-City service per day.

Continue uphill beyond the bridge, on a lovely deep sunken way which broadens out past Moseley Farm, another attractive old farmhouse building perched on what is undoubtedly an ancient, perhaps semi-fortified site on a low, defensive hill above the valley. Follow the track up as it curves back towards the outskirts of Cookridge, soon passing woods and a cricket ground before coming to a well-signed junction. Turn left here along a track which follows and begins to descend the low ridge of Crag Hill. But just above the entrance to Crag Hill Farm, look for a path at a stile, right, which goes above and around the farm, following a low wall, and, over the next stile alongside a hedge as it descends to the massive circular stone air-shaft of Bramhope Tunnel.

This next section of the route follows the line of Bramhope Tunnel. As you approach the tunnel, go through the gate and stile directly ahead, but after barely ten metres, over a narrow wooden stile in the fence on the right which leads to a path, which descends half left to a stone stile by the wood on the left, below the house.

The path, which has been diverted, takes you around the edge of a long overgrown tunnel spoil tip, along an enclosed way between the wooded mound and a fence. As you reach a stile, keep directly ahead to the lane at a bend in the road where there is a stile and a signpost.

Cross carefully (beware of speeding traffic), the path almost directly opposite, well-signed, taking you deep into an area of scrubby woodland, narrow but easy to follow, which eventually opens out into a field. Keep to the left of the next air-shaft looking for the stile diagonally left in the next field, bearing half right now towards another overgrown spoil tip through which the path winds, keeping ahead over scrubland and a stile in a fence to reach another lane.

A footpath sign marks the path continuation cutting across the corner of a field by stiles and then along a track to a cottage before veering left along a well used path through lovely beech woods.

Keep ahead, but where the path forks, keep right onto an enclosed way behind gardens which emerges at Breary Lane in the centre of Bramhope village.

Bramhope has long been absorbed into outer suburban Leeds, pleasant between the wars housing and shops more like Headingley than Wharfedale. But turn left along the street for some 300 metres to the cross roads with its lovely old directional sign, at stage coach height, and directly opposite the Fox and Hounds pub.

To save a little road walking, retrace your steps along Breary Lane to the church where just before and also by the estate agent's shop, there is an entrance into a cul de sac, at the bottom of which a stile leads down steps into an area of informal parkland, below which a kissing gate leads into the main Leeds-Otley road, the A660, close to the entrance to the Forte-Crest Leeds-Bradford Motel.

Cross with care, turning left to pass the hotel entrance to notice, somewhat incongruously, a little chapel on a grassy mound. This is Bramhope Chapel, a rare link with Cromwellian England, built 1649 during the Protectorate. A simple, even austere little building, reflecting its Puritan origins, it's worth looking through its tiny windows to see the massive three-decker pulpit and perfectly preserved box-pews.

From the Chapel, continue along Otley Road, ignoring Hall Drive on the right, but take the less sharp turn down a tarmac lane with a NoThrough Road sign. This is Staircase Lane, an ancient pre-turnpike road which follows the hillside steeply downhill below, past some fine houses and gardens. There are spectacular views of Wharfedale and across to Almscliffe Crags as you descend. Where the road ends, continue straight ahead down a lovely sandy track. This is the ancient road from Knaresborough to Bradford, which goes steeply up the hillside, long predating the later turnpike roads, and was formerly used by packhorses and people on horseback and foot.

The track eventually meets the drive from the entrance and garage of another large house and descends to the main and extremely busy Bradford-Harrogate above Pool. Follow this along the narrow path by the roadside, but after 80 metres, cross with great care to a remarkable stone gateway inscribed "L'Avenue des Hirondelles" – the Avenue of the Swallows.

This is all that remains of a failed speculative venture by an Edwardian builder who bought land and laid out a grand avenue of chestnut trees to sell houses and building plots and build houses overlooking the Wharfe valley. Some houses were built and sold and remain as fine dwellings, but the First World War intervened and the scheme failed, with only a few smaller houses being added, and the Avenue of the Swallows petering out in green fields – and no doubt the haunt of swallows.

Follow the drive under the archway and uphill, between the chestnuts, keeping straight ahead as the avenue curves to the left and ends, heading over a stile and keeping ahead (more fine views) to a stile into woods. This enters a long disused, long overgrown quarry, a lovely area of woodland. The path bears slightly to the right, then climbs steeply past overgrown quarry faces to emerge at Far Row, a row of quarrymen's cottages. Follow the drive past the cottages to the left until it emerges at the little toll keeper's cottage at Pool Bar – one of the few to survive, at the top of Pool Bank on the A660. This was the first turnpike road built in the 18th century to replace Staircase Lane, before being replaced in turn by the 19th century Killinghall-Dudley Hill (Bradford) turnpike road which is still in use as the Bradford-Harrogate road.

In the corner of the stone wall opposite the tollbooth cottages, a gap stile leads to a path (signed), leading to a narrow path which follows the hillside downhill towards Caley Hall Farm ahead. The path crosses open scrubland below a wood, before bearing slightly right down the hillside to join a much more distinct track by the wall and rowan trees below. Keep left here, but soon entering Caley Hall by a gate and into the farmyard where the path, on the left (signed) takes the walker to the north and around the outside of the terraced gardens of the Hall. Stiles lead to the path across the farm drive, bearing slightly right to the wall corner, then following along wall and hedge. Keep along this way following waymarks to where the path goes underneath the embankment of the old railway line;

then the path continues sharp left over a stile alongside the embankment before emerging on a track.

Turn right here for some 50 metres to where there is a stile on the left, to the houses which are visible across the playing field directly ahead. Make for the nearest house near where a small gate and narrow way leads into a housing estate. Keep ahead in the estate road to the first junction, turning first right and then first left along Cambridge Way which leads into the main road continuing, to the right, into the centre of Otley, with its choice of inns and, on the left, the bus station with frequent buses to Leeds, Bradford and Ilkley.

If you are interested in the stone Memorial to the men who died building Bramhope Tunnel mentioned above, you can find it close by the Parish Church, in the little extension to the churchyard beyond the footpath.

Walk 16: The Fly Line, Aberford and Lotherton Hall

An eight-mile circular walk through the gentle rolling countryside that forms Leeds' eastern fringe, taking in the route of an historic railway line, a fine old coaching town and one of Leeds' most delightful museums and country parks.

Distance: 12km (8 mls)

Maps: Landranger 105; Pathfinder 684

Start and Finish (circular): Garforth Railway Station

Getting there: MetroTrain York or Selby lines to Garforth Station. Motorists should park at or near Garforth Station. Public transport users can shorten the walk by a little over half a mile (1km) by returning from East Garforth Station. There are also frequent return buses from Aberford to Cross Gates and Leeds and, on Sundays, an hourly service (summer only) from Lotherton Hall (service 56) should you decide to shorten the walk from there.

The Pubs

The White Swan in Aberford (0113 281 3205) is a famous Yorkshire 18th century coaching inn with bow windows, low beams and a massive courtyard and stables where a painted sign still offers fast post horses for stage coaches. Now a hotel and restaurant, there is a comfortable but not over modernised bar that welcomes walkers – with Boddingtons, Tetley Bitter, Whitbread Trophy (cask) and Castle Eden on offer, as well as bar meals. Open all day most days.

    The Blands Arms in Old Micklefield (0113 286 2465) is quite different in character – a typical small village pub, dating from the middle of last century, unpretentious but with character – friendly landlady welcoming walkers, excellent Sam Smiths Old Brewery Bitter and good value bar meals. Open until 4pm on most days.

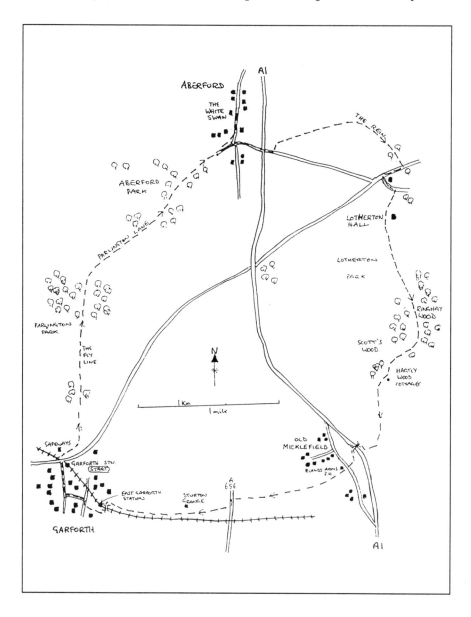

The Walk

From Garforth Station's eastbound platform exit, turn right along the busy A642 to the pedestrian lights. Cross and turn right past the Safeway supermarket, turning left past the entrance into Lotherton Way, an industrial estate road past small factories and warehouses, following it to the right past more industrial buildings to where it ends at a junction of tracks. Turn right at the end, but almost immediately turn sharp left as you reach a second junction. The track, signposted "The Fly Line", follows a long fence past a concrete works before becoming a narrow, brick surfaced track heading in a straight line almost due northwards, past woods and into open countryside.

The Fly Line was a remarkable industrial and passenger railway. It was built in the 1830s by Richard Gascoigne, owner of Parlington Hall, to link two collieries on his estates, the Elizabeth and Isabella pits, with the newly opened Leeds-Selby railway at Garforth. Passenger services began in 1834, using a rather primitive four wheeled carriage built in the colliery workshops and known as the "High Flyer" – hence "Fly Line". A horse was the motive power, but the trains were powered by gravity down the long and gentle incline through Parlington Park back to Garforth, with the horse travelling in style in the dandy cart, before hauling the carriage back uphill on the return trip.

Steam engines were introduced in 1870 and eventually there was a daily service between Aberford and Garforth, with a fare of 3d (1¼p) single and 6p (2½p) return second class, and 9p (3p) first class return. Astonishingly the Fly Line survived as a passenger railway as late at March 1924 with a market-day only service still operating before it finally yielded to motor bus competition.

The old railway line was finally claimed as a public right of way after a prolonged legal battle and it now provides a delightful walk through the estate, the gentle gradient through rolling countryside no hardship as you pass Hawks Nest Farm where there was a former engine shed and Lily Pit Cottages. Soon the Fly Line enters dense woodland, Parlington Hollins, with chestnut, birch, oak, sycamore and ash trees, passing under an old archway, known as Light Arch, then bears to the right, still through dense woodland to eventually emerge at a junction of bridle-paths at Keeper's House.

Bear right along the main track with the bridleway signs. This track, known as Parlington Lane, soon goes under a rather atmospheric but fairly well lit tunnel and skirts the edge of Parlington Park, through tall, mature beech woods. Keep ahead through the entrance gate and on into Aberford village.

The Great North Road – the A1 – no longer roars its way through Aberford, and has left the town in a rather delightful time warp. Aberford was one of a chain of once busy towns which served the huge traffic of stage coaches and mail coaches that thundered between London and Edinburgh. Lovely honey-coloured magnesium limestone give the villages a Cotswold flavour, and the main street of old shops and houses (many of them former inns) is full of atmosphere. To your right is a remarkable row of neo-Gothic almshouses, like miniature houses of Parliament, built by the Gascoigne family in 1844 to house poor people in the parish. There is even a fine old windmill tower overlooking the village.

Turn left and walk through the village for the White Swan is at the top, or north side of the village, at the corner of the lane to Thorner.

Return, suitably refreshed, back to the junction with the Lotherton Road, opposite Parlington Lane. Keep on the footway on the far side to go under the large concrete viaduct bridge carrying the present A1, before taking the first turning on the left, Stockinger Lane. This looks like a through road but is really a cul-de sac leading to a farm. Follow it as it bends to the right between open fields for about half a mile – a kilometre – until you reach a long, narrow wood, which is in fact growing around an ancient earthwork known as The Rein, believed to be an Iron Age defensive fortification. The Rein crosses the lane where the lane turns left. At the far side of The Rein is a gate on the right which leads to a path which follows a narrow track alongside The Rein. Keep in the same direction following the Rein for about a mile (1.5km) until a busy lane is reached at a gate. Turn right here, keeping on the wide verge for 250 metres to a junction at

Lotherton Farm. Cross this fairly busy and fast road with care to turn left into this quieter lane past the Farm, but after 100 metres, at a bend in the road, go through the gate on the right which leads into the main car park at Lotherton Hall. Cross directly across the car park and pass (or go into) the famous Bird Garden and on to the Hall itself.

Lotherton Hall is a delightful country park and house that its owner, Leeds City Council, is justly proud of. Given to the city in 1968 by Sir Alvary Gascoigne (1893-1970), of the same family who owned Parlington Park, and a former British Ambassador to both Japan, the USSR and China, this lovely Edwardian house with its exquisite gardens now houses not only the original Gascoigne collections, but major Leeds City collections of jewellery, ceramics, silverware, furniture and paintings, including a remarkable Oriental Gallery and a costume gallery. Muddy boots may have to be left in the entrance. There is also a tea room in the old stables with light refreshments, snacks, toilets, a Norman church, Japanese and Italian gardens, a rockery, a wild garden, the Bird Garden, woodland walks and splendid wild gardens.

The walk continues along the south of the house following the Coburnhill Wood signs which lead from the south west corner of the gardens and then on through a kissing gate through a small enclosure of rare breed cattle. Keep directly ahead along the field edge path once again in lovely open countryside, heading to and through the wood. At a cross roads in the wood, keep directly ahead. But as you emerge at the southern edge and open field, take the path to the right, which soon becomes a track. This follows the outside of Scots Wood, following the track and wood to the left after 400 metres, then right around West Wood before turning left and due south once again. Still on a clear track, it climbs slowly uphill on a low ridge for about 500 metres to a T-junction opposite farm buildings, Hartley Wood Cottages.

Turn right here, now heading to the A1, turning right again alongside the motorway to locate a footbridge. Turn left at the far side of the bridge, then right up to the lane in Micklefield, with Blands Arms on the left.

The route continues along the signed path between the Bland Arms and the Primary School, continuing past the school playing field and along a grassy headland path between ploughed fields for around 400 metres to a T- junction at a crossing track where you turn right, but after ten metres, sharp left along a path which is far from clear, but runs on or alongside an overgrown headland between ploughed fields. Where the headland ends is the remains of a stile. Cross the field directly behind (which may be ploughed but there should be a clear path marked out), keeping the same direction to where in the fence alongside the main A565 road you'll find a stile and metal footpath sign.

Cross the main road carefully, turning left for 100 metres and walking along the verge to the entrance to Sturton Grange Farm where a footpath (signed) on the right indicates a farm track parallel to the railway. Continue in the same direction past the point where the track swings right to the farm, to where the path goes over a stile alongside the railway, ignoring the bridge over the railway on the left. Follow the field path over stiles alongside the railway fence to the edge of Garforth and the bus turning circle at East Garforth Station. Cross the railway by the footbridge to the Leeds-bound platform.

Frequent trains run from here back to Leeds, but to return to a parked car or to Garforth Station for a better choice of trains (especially on Sundays), turn right outside the station exit, walking along the lane to a junction, before turning right again and then taking the first road left, Church Lane. Pass the church and St. Mary's Hall on the left, then turn right into Station Fields, a road past a school, which leads directly to Garforth Station.

Walk 17: The Kingdom of Elmet – Barwick and Thorner

This ramble links two popular villages east of Leeds, Barwick and Thorner, and explores the fertile countryside which in the past sheltered a tiny independent Celtic Kingdom – Elmet.

Distance: 10km (6 mls)

Maps: Landranger 104; Pathfinders 672, 693

Start & Finish (circular walk): Barwick in Elmet village

Getting There: Bus 56 from Tinshill, Headingley and Eastgate or 64 from Leeds City Square to Barwick. Motorists should park in Barwick.

The Pub

The Fox Inn, Thorner (0113 289 2489). A popular, friendly pub, in a typical Victorian building fronting onto Thorner's picturesque Main Street. Very much a village local – unpretentious, with a comfortable bar, and choice of reasonably priced food most lunchtimes. Beer, John Smiths Bitter and Magnet, is very well-kept.

The Walk

Barwick in Elmet is reputed to have once been the capital of the tiny kingdom of Elmet – an enclave of Celtic civilisation which continued to flourish during Anglian times, well into the 8th century. It was perhaps a relic of the former Kingdom of Brigantia, defeated by the Romans in the first century, but one which remained as a semi-autonomous Romano-British settlement on the well-drained and fertile magnesium limestone foothills between the River Aire and the Vale of York. Little archaeological evidence of the Celtic

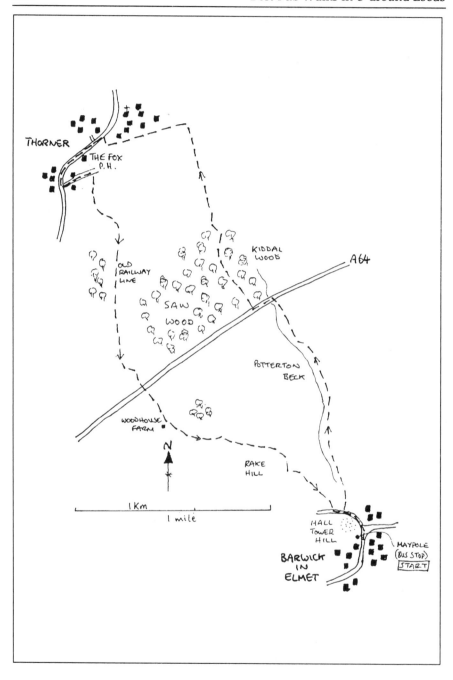

THORNER

THE FOX
P.H.

KIDDAL
WOOD

A64

OLD
RAILWAY
LINE

SAW
WOOD

POTTERTON
BECK

WOODHOUSE
FARM

N

RAKE
HILL

1 Km

1 mile

HALL
TOWER
HILL

MAYPOLE
(BUS STOP)
START

BARWICK
IN
ELMET

kingdom remains, save for earthworks around Aberford which may have been a defensive fortification against Anglian invasion. and the tall green hillock behind the chapel and graveyard, known as Hall Tower Hill – best seen from the graveyard – which may have been a castle or fortified palace of the Kings of Elmet. Whether the community simply integrated with its Anglian neighbours or was overwhelmed by later Danish invasion is not clear – the name Barwick suggests a later Norse settlement on the site. All Saints Church has a window dating back to Norman times, and fragments of two Anglo-Saxon crosses.

Start at the Gascoigne Arms (bus stop close by) by Barwick in Elmet's ancient maypole and walk down the lane known as The Boyle. Follow this to the right round past the chapel and Tower Hill. Where The Boyle swings sharp left, keep straight ahead along a track descending to a footbridge over Rake Beck. Cross and follow this enclosed track northwards which forms part of the well-waymarked Leeds Country Way. Keep ahead, ignoring a track on the left, then continue to the end of the track. Go over a stile, continuing over a low hillock, with a hedge on your left, before again descending to a footbridge, this time crossing Potternewton Beck at Copple Syke Spring. Follow the grassy lane along a shallow valley, passing another spring called Jacob's Well, then through a field gate to emerge at the embankment carrying the busy A64 York Road by Kiddal Bridge.

Turn left along the footpath which slopes up the embankment and cross the A64 with extreme care, and follow the clear path opposite which leads through Kiddal Wood. Keep ahead on the main path through the wood. As the path reaches the end of the wood and bends left, keep on the Leeds Country Way, bearing right to follow a path between the fences. Keep ahead through a gate into a walled green lane. This emerges at a track behind houses and gardens. Turn left here keeping ahead at a junction along an unmetalled way which emerges at the south side of Thorner Green at Stead Lane.

Cross an attractive expanse of the Green and join Main Street to the west of the church. Follow Main Street with its pleasant rows of Georgian and Victorian cottages to the Fox Inn.

From the pub follow the same direction along Main Street past the point as the road curves to the left, passing the lane on the right that crosses Thorner's much photographed ford. At about 80 metres beyond this junction, look for a narrow enclosed path left, between garden walls and then beech hedges. Follow this for a little less than a hundred metres before turning right along a similar enclosed way. This soon goes over a crossing track – maintain the same direction as it squeezes by gardens, then bears left, over a stile into an open field. Turn right over the next stile into a long field. The right of way goes down this next enlarged field, but most walkers head for a stile on the left which leads to a well-used path along the embankment of the old Leeds-Wetherby railway line. Turn right and follow the embankment with its pleasant elevated views of surrounding woods and meadow for some 600 metres to where the way ahead is blocked; the path going left and then sharp right alongside the embankment. Follow this for 400 metres to a crossing fence. The path follows this fence left before turning right around an enclosure and heading for the A64 road.

Cross carefully, this time following the track which leads down and bears left to Woodhouse Farm. Follow the path which leads past the farm, heading due east with a fence on your left along the edge of a narrow field for 300 metres to a stile and junction of paths. Then keeping the hedge and then a ditch on your right, past a line of isolated trees for a further 400 metres to an old hawthorn tree where the remains of a stile indicates a line of path over the ditch to an isolated tree on the right, still keeping the same direction to a marker post ahead. Turn left here and follow the field boundary with a hedge to your right, following the field edge where it turns right, over a stile in the next field corner, and keeping ahead with the hedge on your right to the next stile ahead by a gate. With the hedge on your left, cross another stile and footbridge over Rake Beck, soon bearing right after a few metres up to a signpost marking the exit stile in the top left-hand corner of the field. Turn left along the road, and follow it as it curves right into the centre of Barwick village.

Walk 18: Bramham Park and Village

Eighteenth century parkland, a still deeply rural village and a now forgotten spa are explored on this nine mile walk through Leeds' richly beautiful "Little Cotswold Country".

Distance: 14.5km (9 mls)

Maps: Landranger 105; Pathfinders 673, 684

Start: Aberford

Finish: Boston Spa

Getting there: Bus service 64 from Leeds City Square to Aberford; return on bus service 760 from Boston Spa. Both services operate half hourly on weekdays and hourly on Sundays.

The Pub

Red Lion, Bramham (01937 843524). At the village cross roads, opposite the War Memorial. This is an 18th century village pub which, though modernised, has kept its essential character – low beams, pleasant tap room, lounge and dining area – with an excellent choice of meals on offer. Sam Smith's Old Brewery Bitter. Closes at 3pm lunchtimes.

The Walk

Alight at the bus stop at Aberford Bridge. Turn left to cross this fine old bridge over Cock Beck past the Arabian Horse (CAMRA listed worth a call) and attractive village green then take the first lane left, Becca Lane, past cottages. This soon goes alongside a steep and thickly wooded embankment, Becca Banks. This is an ancient

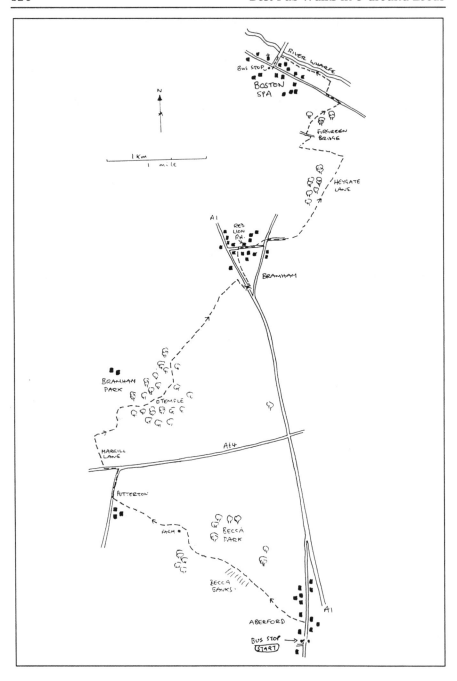

earthwork, and almost certainly Iron Age in origin, perhaps defensive fortifications of the ancient kingdom of Elmet (see walk 17), safeguarding the little Celtic enclave against Anglian attacks from the north. The Ridge continues for some distance to the west.

The lane soon reaches a lodge and park gates. The legend "No Access" is misleading and refers to motor vehicles – this is a public bridleway. Enter the parkland of Becca Park along what is now a stony track, crossing an open area. As Becca Hall comes into view, you approach a junction of paths, with a clear footpath sign and map. The right of way is to the left, around the edge of the wood, along a hedge to a rickety fieldgate. Keep ahead along the track as it curves northwards to Becca House Farm, a large complex. Pass the farm and cottages and about 80 metres north of the farm (not where it is shown on the current maps) look for a yellow diamond waymark on a post. This indicates the line of path which crosses sharply left across a wheatfield, the path clearly protected. More yellow waymarks indicate the line of path towards some trees ahead, crossing a tiny footbridge and curving north by the edge of the field and passing a small woodland. Keep ahead by the wood to stile through the edge of a copse, keeping left along the edge of the field and wood. The next stile is some eight metres from the field corner. Cross and head diagonally across the field towards the pylons where there is a stile and footpath sign.

Turn right into Potterton Lane now closed to traffic, heading to the horrendously busy A64. Turn left here, and head for the cycle warning sign to cross where there are clearer sightlines in both directions – traffic travels at motorway speeds here. Cross and keep in the same direction for another 50 metres to where a bridleway, Mangrill Lane, heads past fields.

Follow this green way for 400 metres to the plantation ahead where pylons cross. Just beyond the pylons a stile and footpath sign, right, leads into an enclosed path, which can be overgrown in summer and muddy in winter. Follow this for another 400 metres to where, soon past a group of young sycamores in the hedge there is a clearing, by pine trees. Turn left here, and along a broad firebreak. Where the wood gives way to an open field on the right, keep ahead to the clump of mature trees ahead to reach a crossing track.

Turn right here. This is an attractive path, soon dipping down into a hollow in the woods. At a fork keep right – look for the yellow waymarks, but after 100 metres at a junction take the track left, signed and waymarked, which leads into the lovely landscape of Bramham Park. Follow the track by the edge of the wood as it gently ascends to a beautiful classical Temple on a little headland, around which the path curves. To the right, partially concealed by trees is Bramham Park House, one of Yorkshire's greatest country houses. It is described as one of the finest examples in England of a landscape garden in the French manner of King Louis XIV. You'll see, partly concealed by the Ionic Temple, a tall stone obelisk at the southern end of the wood.

Follow the track past the Temple and across lovely open parkland, in summer fields fringed by poppies. Left at the first junction, waymarked, and after another 300 metres, right at the next, a long straight path with superb views, the house now in clearer view, as you descend to Bramham village. As you go through the gate into Wellhill Farm, look for the waymarks that direct you left along the track before the farm, and out past the fine 18th century house known as the Priory.

Your ears will already be assaulted by the roaring traffic of the A1 (M). Turn right at the end of the track and ascend to the bridge over the motorway, going first left down the paved path which follows the far side of the motorway. This joins the road into Bramham village, a short cut cutting the corner into the village centre. The Red Lion is at the old cross roads, once busy with stage coaches on the old Great North Road, now spared the frantic pace of the motorway age.

Turn left coming out of the Red Lion along Low Way, keeping left at the fork past the Methodist Church towards the lovely Norman Parish church. Take the path through the churchyard emerging at the gate at the far side. Cross into Vicarage Lane where almost opposite you'll see a short ginnel past gardens which leads into a cul de sac residential road, Prospect Bank. Turn right here, then left

The Red Lion, Bramham

at the junction into Windmill Lane, then first right along Hegate Lane, a narrow, quiet farm road. Keep on this lane as it gradually gets more grassy and finally turns left and becomes a stony track, going underneath pylons. Ignore the first path on the left but continue almost to the gate at the end of the lane where a grassy track, between fences, leads off left. You'll see two churches ahead, in the village of Clifford. The nearest with a massive tower in Grand Romanesque style was built between 1845-8 for a local Catholic family, the Grimstons, with the Pope and the King of France contributed towards the cost. The second, the Parish Church, with a smaller, square tower, was built just a few years earlier in 1841-2

Take this track, back under the pylons but where it curves to the left, take a stile sharply to the right which leads to a grassy way along the edge of a field to another stile left, zigzagging back along an enclosed path which goes around the edge of the field to the lane at Firgreen Bridge. Left here, across the bridge over Carr Beck immediately beyond which there is a stile, leading to a riverside path along the edge of a series of long fields. Following the stiles, the path eventually curves to the right of a pig farm, passing ponds and emerging at a gate at Low Mills Farm. Turn left along the busy A659 towards Boston Spa for 400 metres where, opposite the 30mph sign, a signed path leads to the riverside past gardens and houses.

New bungalows on the riverside have replaced what remained of the old Spa Baths which in turn formed part of the original spa buildings. Mineral rich springs from below the magnesium limestone cliffs by the riverside were favoured for drinking and bathing in as a health cure by travellers arriving by coach on the new turnpike road from York. By the mid 18th century, Boston Spa with its coaching inns was enjoying quite a reputation for its healing waters. Sadly for Boston Spa much more vigorous and varied springs were also being discovered in the marshes at "Haregate" near Knaresborough, and as Harrogate's fame spread, so Boston Spa's declined. But the coaching inns survived as did a lovely old main street of fine old houses and shops, and this forgotten little spa town is a pleasant place to take a rest in, in either coffee house or tavern, or even a fashionable shop or two before the bus.

Follow the pretty riverside path to Boston Spa's lovely old bridge. Turn left up the hill to the town centre. The bus stop for the 760 bus for Leeds is about 40 metres on the right – on the opposite side of the road to the church.

Walk 19: Ledsham

A walk of quite remarkable contrasts – from an old mining village, through a gracious country estate, past a village with a rare and beautiful Anglo-Saxon church, to an immense man-made nature reserve created from the industry of the lower Aire Valley.

Distance: 11km (7 mls)

Maps: Landranger 105; Pathfinders 684, 693

Start: Micklefield Station

Finish: Castleford Station

Getting there: Micklefield can be reached by taking any local stopping Metrotrain service on the York or Selby Lines, whilst all MetroTrain Hallam and Pontefract Line trains serve Castleford to return to Leeds. Motorists should park in Leeds and take the train.

The Pub

The Chequers Inn, Ledsham (01977 683135). Described in the CAMRA Guide as a gem, this lovely ivy-covered 18th century country inn has carved oak panelling and antique settles, a traditional bar, and noted restaurant. Beer garden outside. Beer available includes Theakstons's XB, Younger's Bitter, Scotch Bitter and Younger's No 3.

Note: The Chequers has only a six-day licence (closed Sundays); it also closes weekdays at 3pm until 5.30pm, so outside these times you might have to rely on the Old Mill at Castleford (see below).

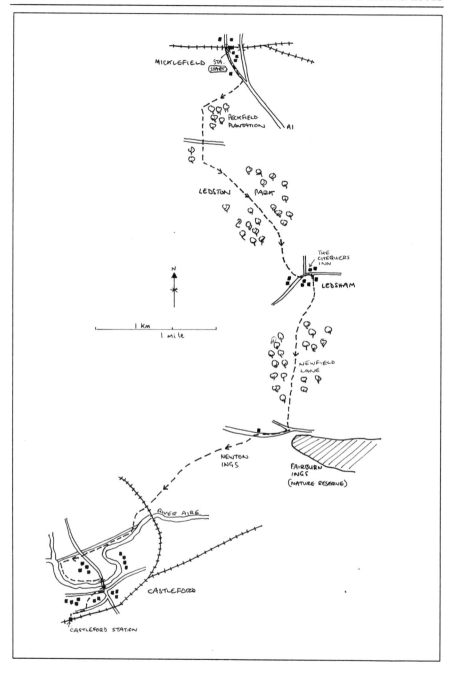

The Walk

From Micklefield Station (which still has a surviving 1840s Leeds-Selby Railway Station-master's house) turn sharp left as you descend to leave the exit from the station, going left again under the bridge and into Micklefield village. This is a coal-mining community that like so many others has lost its mines – the Miners' Welfare Club on the right a sad relic. There are typical "long row" terraces of brick cottages on the left, those on the right are probably older, of mellow, locally quarried magnesium limestone with characteristic long and colourful cottage gardens.

Walk through the village, past the garage, cafe and lorry park, to where, beyond the bungalow, a grassy track on the right, signposted, leads to a wood ahead between fence and field. When you reach the wood turn right. The public path actually goes around the outside of the wood, an area now infringed by the quarry and its waste, so follow the heavily used permissive path which, about 15 metres before the quarry turns left into the wood. Keep to the main path as it bears right to the top and alongside the edge of the wood before meeting a crossing path, (the right of way). Turn left here, but at a fork take the narrower path right, which winds through quite dense vegetation to emerge on the main A63 Selby road at a footpath sign.

Cross with care to continue along the broad track opposite, alongside another wood. Keep ahead to a gate and stile on the left where a path, signed, leads into a plantation of young beech trees. Keep the same direction to another stile which leads into Ledston Park. Your way is due southeast, across open grassland, the line of path indicated by waymarker posts. Head for what seems a gap between the three trees ahead, three massive beech trees marking the line of path, with the towers of Ledston Lodge, a 17th century hunting lodge, appearing on the left. Keep the same direction, but bearing slightly right as you begin to descend, gradually entering a great semi-circle of pasture enclosed by a horseshoe of trees. Look ahead for a stile marked with a yellow marker by a hurdle fence. This leads into a lovely beech wood, and a path which descends through the wood to emerge at a track. Turn left here, following a lane past modern houses into the centre of Ledsham, with The Chequers Inn almost opposite the junction.

Ledsham church

From the inn, cross to All Saints Church in the centre of the village, perhaps taking the paved way through the churchyard to note remains of a tiny 8th century Anglo-Saxon church, whose form and masonry can be still traced, remarkably intact, despite later alterations and enlargements to the building. The church will probably be locked, but if not, it is worth going inside to see Saxon and Norman masonry and an exquisite late 18th century memorial to Lady Betty Hastings, a local lady widely noted for her "intellect and virtue".

From the church path return to the road, but take the cul-de sac lane to the right, signed as a bridle-path. As this heads into a modern cul de sac, the older way is to the left which soon becomes an open track between the fields – Newfield Lane. This is a particularly beautiful ancient way, crossing a deeply rural landscape, with views of Fairburn, the village in the distance, along the valley. Soon colonnaded by trees and alongside a wood, with fine views across the flooded watermeadows which form Fairburn Ings Nature Reserve, the path eventually dips to join Back Newton Lane. Turn left here for a few metres to the cross roads.

Fairburn Ings are a series of artificial lakes or "flashes" in the lower Aire Valley caused by mining subsistence, but now remarkable for the extraordinary variety and quantity of their birdlife – resident and migrant waders, geese, kingfisher, wagtails, making this a bird-watcher's paradise.

Turn right at the junction and walk forward into the RSPB car park and bird reserve, keeping right past the parking and picnic areas. If you decide to explore the reserve, there is a reception kiosk for information and permissive paths radiate from the car park to viewing areas in the Reserve.

Otherwise go through the fieldgate at the far side of the picnic area/car park onto the road and continue in the same direction, walking single file on the narrow verge on the left, for some 200 metres to where, opposite a signed path on the right before Newton Farm, a stile on the left leads down steps. This path has been diverted from that shown on most current maps, but is clearly waymarked by yellow arrows, as it crosses the field diagonally right, towards a waymarked gatepost to the left of marshland. Keep in the same direction to a gate and stile, then alongside a fence on the left to a stile under willow trees; the fence now on the right as you approach the railway line. At the iron pillared railway viaduct, take the path over the little footbridge and then go forward, if it is dry under the arches of the new concrete open cast workings road bridge ahead to make for the embankment along the River Aire (if the area is flooded, keep to the higher embankment to cross the road). Ahead is the lock keeper's cottage at Bullholme Lock. Cross by the foot-bridge over the locks with care, turning right along the grassy embankment on the other side. You will see a variety of craft at this point, including pleasure boats and if you are lucky, a large industrial barge heading on to Goole or Hull. This is the Aire and Calder Navigation, Yorkshire's most important commercial waterway.

Pass moorings and a chemical works to enter a yard and garaging area – bear left past the Navigation Offices to join the main Barnsdale Road into Castleford.

There are two pubs on the corner – **The Griffin** (John Smiths) and opposite **The Old Mill**, the latter with a good choice of Theakston's mild and XB and Younger's Bitter, compensation if you had arrived at The Chequers on the wrong day.

For a nicer way into Castleford than the industrial main road, cross behind the Old Mill past a beer garden and playground over an open area of recreational ground, towards the terraced housing on the left, continuing along the narrow street past allotments to join the river bank, and walk along the flood bank above the River Aire to Castleford's handsome stone bridge, crossing the line of a Roman Road, passing Allinson's Stone Ground Flour Water Mill by Castleford Weir.

The path leads into a street. Follow the street to Castleford Bridge and cross the river. Little remains of the Roman fort guarding the ford over the River Aire apart from a few fragments of Roman pottery and earthenware in the town's little museum above the library. Turn right at the junction past the bridge past the Ship Inn, crossing the road at the refuge, then left up Sagar Street, turning right into and through the recently pedestrianised Carlton Street. Keep straight ahead at the end of the pedestrian zone, before turning first left directly to Castleford station.

Walk 20: Wetherby to Spofforth

The old coaching town of Wetherby on the River Wharfe is rich in character and history. This walk gives the chance to explore the old town with its choice of historic inns, riverside walks and a railway trail that leads deep into the local countryside.

Distance: 14km (9 mls)

Maps: Landrangers 104, 105; Pathfinders 684, 693

Start and Finish (circular walk): Wetherby

Public Toilets: In the town centre by the Shambles

Getting there: Bus 98 from Leeds Infirmary Street (direct) or 760 from Leeds Bus Station via Bramham/Boston Spa (longer journey) Motorists should park in Wetherby – large choice of free car parks.

The Pubs

The Crown, Wetherby (01937 584402) A typical market town pub, large, roomy and pleasantly old fashioned with a pool room at the back and comfortable lounge and bar area to the front. Sam Smith's Old Brewery Bitter. Food at lunchtimes.

The Railway Inn, Spofforth (01937 590257) [reached by direct path from the Harland Way railway path] is a friendly, village pub with a comfortable bar. There's also an extremely attractive beer garden outside which welcomes families. Sam Smith's Old Brewery Bitter. Food usually available.

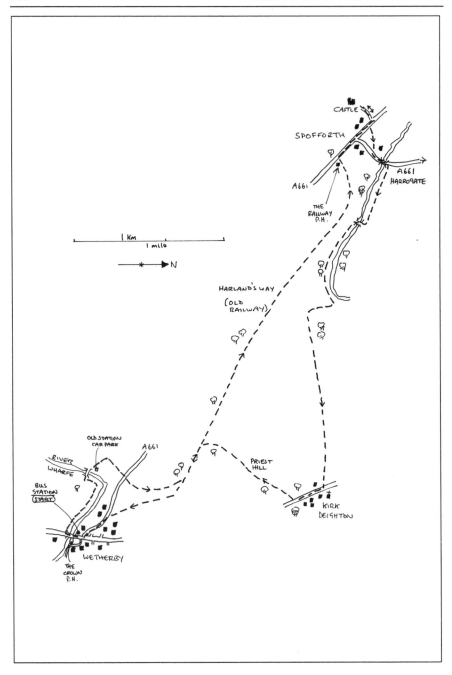

Wetherby Town Hall

The Walk

Make sure you give yourself plenty of time, perhaps at the end of this walk, to explore Wetherby – a delightful old town, full of charming narrow streets, alleyways, courts, a picturesque town hall, and shambles. Like its neighbour Tadcaster downstream, Wetherby owes its attractive cream coloured walls and buildings to the bedrock of magnesium limestone. Local springs produce hard, mineral-rich water – which is ideal for brewing, and like Tadcaster, Wetherby was once famous for its breweries as well as its race-course. The race-course remains but the breweries have now gone, no doubt owing to the competition from down river, but there's at least Tadcaster-brewed Sam Smiths to be had both in Wetherby and nearby Spofforth reached on this walk.

From Wetherby Bus Station or town centre car parks, make your way down to and across Wetherby's fine old bridge, noting the

The Crown

medieval dam across the River Wharfe, which for centuries provided a head of water to power the town's corn mill.

Turn right at the far side of the bridge towards the new Swimming Pool, continuing beyond the pool and car park to where a stile leads to the path along the flood bank. Follow the river upstream and around the gentle bend behind the town, past the site of the long vanished medieval castle on the headland opposite, to the relatively new footbridge. Cross the bridge and head for the steps slightly to the right to join the road. Turn left for some 50 metres to the entrance to the car park on the site of Wetherby's former railway station – one of the very first victims of Beeching's axe. Part of the railway line has been developed into what is now the Harland Way, a three mile walking and cycle path between Wetherby and Spofforth.

Bear right at the start of the Way in a deep cutting, and where the track forks, at what was known as the "Wetherby Triangle" bear left, still in the cutting, the track swinging northwestwards to join the former line from Tadcaster.

Easy, relaxed walking now over the next 6km – 2¼ miles, through a tree-fringed cutting and then a gentle embankment, the latter with open views, to the village of Spofforth. Before the track peters out into an estate road, look for a little narrow way, with a friendly sign, welcoming walkers and cyclists to the Station Inn with its large beer garden.

To explore Spofforth Castle, a focal point for any walk, turn right along the main A661 road through the village centre to where the main road bends sharp right. Your route is directly ahead for another 200 metres following the brown signs, until you reach a narrow path enclosed around a playing field which leads directly to the Castle.

Really more a large fortified house than a castle, this surprisingly extensive ruin dates from the 14th century when Henry Percy, ancestor of Shakespear's Hotspur, was given permission to crenellate or fortify his house. Built from fine red sandstone, the remains of a Tower and the Kitchen, and Great Hall with 15th century windows can be seen. Owned by the village of Spofforth but in the care of English Heritage, the Castle is open at all times during hours of daylight.

To return back to Wetherby, go back to the lane from the Castle entrance path, turning right but then take the first lane left to a T-junction. Turn right here to the village's pretty but tucked away village green and church, and handsome Georgian vicarage. Bear left past the church to rejoin the main road. Cross with care and follow the road over the bridge across the little River Crimple at the far side of which a footpath, signed, leads over a stile down steps to the banks of the river, really no more than a stream. Follow the riverside path, which can be overgrown in late summer, along scrubby embankment for 600 metres to where a partially concealed footbridge takes you over the stream to the other bank. The path continues past somewhat rank vegetation, eventually leading along the top of an extended concrete sewer pipe which curves close to and eventually away from the Harland Way. After a further kilometre, the path crosses a beck by a stile, a little footbridge and pedestrian gate. Turn right here for another 200 metres, until a somewhat clearer path joins at a T-junction. Turn sharp left here, the path broadening to a farmtrack which leads up the low ridge past the farm and into Kirk Deighton.

Kirk Deighton is a charming village with an extremely attractive cottage-lined main street leading up to a rather fine parish church whose tall spire dominates the landscape for some distance around. Sadly, the village also suffers from the noise pollution from the nearby A1 Motorway.

Having explored the village, follow the main street straight downhill until it bends to the left, where a farmtrack leads directly ahead. Take this. Where it forks after 400 metres, take the left fork which ascends Priest Hill to rejoin the Harland Way path. Turn left here, soon reaching the junction and picnic area on the Wetherby triangle, but this time keep straight ahead, along the top side of the triangle.

You can follow the railway path right through to its present eastern terminus in North Street, which is only a short walk (along a busy road) from the town centre, but a pleasanter way into town is to take the first path on the right by the children's play area, before the overbridge, which slopes up by a hedge to a long field. Keep ahead along the field and hedge to join a track which leads into a quiet road past Wetherby's little cinema. Go straight ahead into Westgate and turn left into the centre of town for refreshment, shops, bus station and car parks.

BEST PUB WALKS ON TYNESIDE

This collection of twenty walks is from local authors Lydia Speakman and Richard Baker. There are walks on both sides of the Tyne – alongside, over and even *under* the river! The routes pass through a variety of countryside, often using the network of old waggonways and disused railways. The strong historical flavour provides a real insight into the history of the North East. All of the walks are accessible by public transport, including the Tyne & Wear Metro system. The pubs offer Real Ale and many are CAMRA listed. There is a section on the region's favourite ales as well as some of the more unusual brews. £6.95

WALKING THE CHEVIOTS:
classic circular routes

The walks in this book provide an excellent introduction to this lonely, wild countryside – a true wilderness area. Each route is full of interest, with details of the natural history, geology and archaeology of the area. Many of the walks follow old drove roads, smuggling routes and Roman roads which cross the hills and have been used for centuries. On each walk an exciting and varied day is assured, whatever your ability. Edward Baker has travelled the length and breadth of the Cheviots planning and recording these walks. £7.95

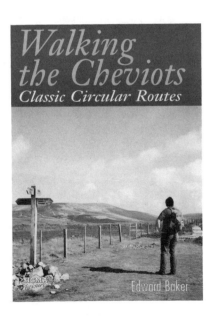

Also of interest ...

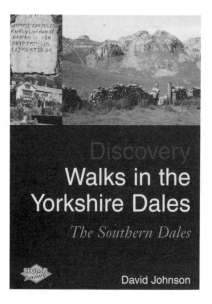